THE GREAT DANE

THE GREAT DANE

JEAN LANNING

POPULAR DOGS

London Melbourne Auckland Johannesburg

Popular Dogs Publishing Co. Ltd

An imprint of Century Hutchinson Ltd
Brookmount House, 62–65 Chandos Place,
London WC2N 4NW

Century Hutchinson Publishing Group (Australia) Pty Ltd
16–22 Church Street, Hawthorn, Melbourne, Victoria 3122

Century Hutchinson Group (NZ) Ltd
32–34 View Road, PO Box 40–086, Glenfield, Auckland 10

Century Hutchinson Group (SA) Pty Ltd
PO Box 337, Bergvlei 2012, South Africa

First published 1971
Second edition 1974
Third edition 1977
Fourth edition 1980
Fifth edition 1986

Printed and bound in Great Britain by
Anchor Brendon Ltd, Tiptree, Essex
ISBN 0 09 161440 6

To all Great Danes, and
those who love the breed

ACKNOWLEDGEMENTS

I should like to acknowledge my debt to those who have been kind in helping me with information and advice on this book.

I am very grateful to Mr. C. A. Binney, Secretary of the Kennel Club, and to members of the club staff, who have been most kind and helpful. Two of our senior judges and breeders, Mr. W. G. Siggers and Miss H. M. Osborn, have helped me to collect photographs of some of the most famous and influential Great Danes of the pre-war era. I am also indebted to Miss Nancy Carroll Draper of the U.S.A. for allowing me to reproduce Maud Earl's famous painting which she now owns, and to Mr. G. N. Gould, C.B.E., Ll.D., F.R.C.V.S., J.P., who gave much of his valuable time to assist on the technical side of the chapter on ailments.

I should also like to express my gratitude to Mrs. B. Douglas Redding for checking the manuscript and proofs, and to Mrs. Shakespeare for typing the first draft of the copy.

Finally, I should like to thank all the breeders who supplied photographs, and the writers past and present who have contributed directly or indirectly to this book.

J.L.

CONTENTS

ILLUSTRATIONS
Between pages 32 and 33

Ch. Fergus of Clausentum
Bred and owned by Mrs. H. A. Lanning and the author

Ch. Rebeller of Ouborough
Bred and owned by the late Mr. J. V. Rank

Nero
Owned by the later Herr E. Messter

Merle Great Dane. Painting by Maud Earl

Lord Topper

Ch. Hannabal of Redgrave

Fauna Moguntia, Ch. Dolf v.d. Saalburg and
   Ch. Bosko v.d. Saalburg
Bred and owned by the late Herr Karl Färber

Ch. Dolf v.d. Saalburg
Bred and owned by the late Herr Karl Färber

Ger. and Am. Ch. Etfa v.d. Saalburg
Bred and owned by the late Herr Karl Färber

Between pages 64 and 65

Grand Ch. Rex Lendor von Zeltnerschloss of Ouborough
Owned by the late Mr. J. V. Rank

Ch. Record of Ouborough
Owned by the late M. J. V. Rank

Group of the famous Send Great Danes

Jean Lanning with a group of Clausentums

Ch. Sarzec Blue Baron
Bred by Mrs. E. Walshe and Mrs. J. Le Coyne
Owned by Mr. and Mrs. B. Craig

Int. Ch. Kaptain of Kilcroney
Bred and owned by Mrs. J. Le Coyne

Ch. Daneton Amilia
Bred by Mr. and Mrs. Butcher
Owned by Mr. and Mrs. M. Duckworth

Ch. Clausentum Magnus
   Bred by the author
   Owned by Mr. P. and Mrs. M. Howell and the author

Ch. Clausentum Gulliver
   Bred by the author
   Owned by Mr. and Mrs. J. Butcher and Mrs. H. A. Lanning

IN THE TEXT

Author's Introduction

When writing this book I endeavoured always to take into account the various schools of thought, bearing in mind that there is always more than one viewpoint on any subject.

Although speaking from personal experience extending over twenty-five years, I am the first to acknowledge that on many important issues such as feeding and exercising there are those who will hold different ideas from mine. There is no short cut to success, but if this book serves to further your ambition to breed better Great Danes, and at the same time stimulates your thinking, then it will have achieved its main objective.

I sincerely hope that those of you who choose to breed Great Danes in the future will do so with a certain amount of pride and humility. The Great Dane is the most handsome and noble of breeds, and there is pride of achievement in bringing him to that high standard of excellence when he is particularly pleasing to the most discerning eye. Moreover, the breeder with humility is always prepared to acknowledge the good specimen, no matter to whom he may belong or how he may be bred. Breeders who are uncharitable in their outlook have narrow vision, and any success they may achieve will consequently be limited. It is all too easy for a breeder to become selfish and breed to a type he prefers. Nobody is interested in what *you* prefer or like; there is only *one* correct type, that which the standard calls for, and the standard must therefore remain our blueprint for constant reference.

My researches revealed that the early German and British breeders had this spirit to a marked degree. A dedicated group of people, their sole aim was the betterment of the breed. Dog breeding in this day and age has not escaped commercialism, which has to a large extent hindered progress; so often the money has become more important than the breed.

Since the introduction is usually written last, one is able to reflect on the contents of the book, and add any items of importance which may have been missed. My thoughts now turn to our breed clubs. From time to time most breeds go through difficult stages, and it seems to me that when this happens the breed clubs should take an interest, and offer guidance where necessary. At present the main purpose of a breed club seems to be to organise dog shows, and while we certainly do not want to see a stituation arise where the clubs dictate to the breeders, there are times when I feel they should assume a certain responsibility, and issue directives through their committees to ensure that a high standard of breeding is constantly aimed for. Owners of stud dogs should be encouraged to be far more selective in the bitches they accept for mating, and there are many other guide lines which could be set down by the clubs.

I have enjoyed writing this book. Great Danes have introduced me to many friends, and my interest in the breed has taken me to foreign lands which I might not otherwise have seen.

Lastly, I would like to urge that you follow a policy where you are always prepared to put far more into the breed than you expect to take out. In this way you will be more than repaid, and have many years of joy and pleasure.

1971   J.L.

Very few revisions are required to this second edition, but the appendices have been extended and brought up to date where necessary. I have also replaced three of the blocks with photographs of outstanding dogs which have been shown since this book was first published.

1974   J.L.

The third edition needs little revision. Having re-read the book recently I was amazed how many of the comments made by early breeders apply so closely to the breed and its fanciers today. I would say that without doubt the brindles and fawns in particular have shown the improvement of the introduction of imported blood; their blending with the leading English lines is in fact producing a type of Great Dane that could be matched against the best of other countries.

Two new photographs of outstanding dogs which have become champions since the second edition appeared have been included in this edition. I have again revised and extended the appendices and amended Kennel Club fees where necessary.

1977 J.L

The fourth edition I feel needs little revision. Prices have had to be brought up-to-date with inflation. It remains a worry to serious breeders that too many poorly bred and poorly reared puppies are still being put on the market. The sad thing is that these unfortunate dogs so often end up as unwanted sick animals, which have eventually to be destroyed. Do not breed a litter unless you are able to rear the puppies well and be able to sell them to the right homes. To breed, wean and sell a litter of large-breed puppies is today a very expensive exercise, on which one is very lucky to break even.

I have completely altered my views on the removal of dew claws (see page 115). We appear to be the only country in the world which finds this necessary. I feel it is merely a cosmetic operation and no particularly useful purpose is served by it. However, back dew claws (rarely found) are unsightly and should always be removed.

In the United Kingdom I feel that our best Great Danes continue to improve and that the rest of the world is again looking to this country for good show and breeding stock.

1980 J.L.

Now going into the fifth edition, there is still no need for any major revision, other than to up-date the appendices where necessary. As I travel around the world, judging our lovely breed and hearing the comments of other Dane enthusiasts, it seems that the original manuscript could have been written only yesterday and still applies today.

Sadly, far too many puppies are still produced, often poorly reared, destined to have short life spans and not enjoy the good health which should be the birthright of every healthy puppy.

The very good imports, which have now been coming into the United Kingdom for almost two decades, have continued to have their influence. Stock acquired from the best American and Swedish breeders, has been of a very high standard of excellence. I would say with confidence that we now have some of the finest Great Danes in the world. But the spur must always be to breed them better still. As ever, breeders must be watchful and continue to breed selectively with discrimination. Rome was not built in a day. Neither are the best Great Danes!

1986   J.L.
Sherfield English,
Romsey, Hampshire

Great Dane History

How long has the Great Dane been with us? The big fawn dog, ancestor of the present Great Dane though heavier in build and more like the Mastiff in type, has been known to mankind throughout the centuries in most parts of the world. It is probable that the Mastiff and the Great Dane had common ancestors, and only after decades of selective breeding has the 'Apollo of all breeds' evolved as we know it today.

The naturalist Buffon was the first to refer to the giant fawn dog as the *Grand Danois*, describing him as the true descendant of the Molossian Dog and the Alaunts. He used the name *Grand Danois* to distinguish from the *Petit Danois*, similar in appearance but smaller.

The *Petit Danois* is considered by some experts to be connected with the Dalmatian; it is interesting to note that people who have kept both breeds frequently refer to Dalmatians as 'little Danes', the two breeds having similarities of temperament and habit.

Writers have long connected and compared the Dalmatian and the Great Dane, from Youatt (1854) and Stonehenge (1876) to Ash, who as recently as 1927 included Dalmatians and Great Danes in a single chapter. Other than conformation, however, the two breeds have no resemblance. The spotting of the Dalmatian and the patches of the harlequin Dane are quite different, although some reference to the earlier Dalmatians describes them as being hound-like and patched. I feel this is a mere coincidence, and that the Great Dane is not directly related to the Dalmatian.

Assyrian huntsmen were known to have large smooth-coated hunting dogs, and in *The Natural History of the Dog*, by Richard and Alice Fiennes, there is an illustration of Assyrian huntsmen around 600 B.C. In Volume II of *The Dog Book*, by James Watson Heinemann, there is a further illustration of the Alaunts with Gaston Poebos and his huntsmen. These dogs are described as being 28–31 in. in size at the withers, and Richardson—writing in 1848—describes them as being gigantic and 30–32 in. at the withers.

From excavations we know that Dane-like dogs existed in Russia, Poland and Middle Germany. The Romans were highly cultured people who traded for fine goods of silver and ivory with the Assyrians, and it is quite likely that the large dogs the latter used were imported through the same channels.

The Romans were interested in raising pure-bred dogs for blood sports, and required the more slimly built animals for this purpose. The British dogs which they imported were famous in that day, and were said to be 'able to break the neck of an ox'. The Roman emperors had a special official called the Procurator Cynogie; he lived in Winchester, known at that time as the City of Dogs, and his job was to procure the best possible specimens to send back to Rome.

Dalziel tells us that long before the Roman Conquest there were dogs closely resembling Great Danes in this country; brought to these islands by the Saxons to hunt wild boar, they can later be seen as Alaunts in illustrations of fourteenth- and fifteenth-century hunting scenes. Buffon and Sydenham Edwards provide the first English information on the breed, saying that his disappearance from this country was due to his propensity to fight his own kind.

The Lyme Mastiffs, which were far more like Great Danes than Mastiffs in appearance, were famous in the sixteenth and seventeenth centuries. Bred at Lyme Park, the home of the Legh family for 600 years (1346–1946), these dogs were greatly prized and were deemed fit for presentation to the royal courts of Europe at that time, but unfortunately they died out in the nineteenth century. From the picture of the Lyme Mastiff which may now be seen at Lyme Hall one can see a striking resemblance to the Great Dane. It seems quite likely that this unique, handsome breed of dog belonging to the beautiful Lyme Park—now the property of the National Trust—had a profound influence on the early development of the Great Dane.

During the Middle Ages these Dane-like dogs were to be found in large numbers in Europe. Wealthy lords and princes formed large hunting packs to hunt the wild boar which then roamed the forests, and they became known as Boar Hounds. One can still see many fine paintings and illustrations showing a wild-boar hunt in progress.

Some of the dogs were badly mutilated in the hunt, and it was for this reason that their ears were first cropped, to avoid them being torn or ripped. Many of the early boar hounds had their ears cut off, but as time passed the cropping became more artistic until we now have the 'long crop' so admired in the United States and on the Continent.

When chasing the boar, the hounds had to pull their quarry to the ground by hanging relentlessly to the boar's ears and eventually dragging down the enraged beast. This old instinct still persists, and when a Dane is excited he will quite often grab your hand or sleeve in a friendly manner. The owner is accustomed to this, but the stranger may find the characteristic somewhat alarming!

The English dogs—long-legged, strong animals—were bred by the aristocracy in the fifteenth and sixteenth centuries, and became great favourites in the royal courts. Numerous English hounds were imported to Germany and crossed with the native boar hound.

In the seventeenth and eighteenth centuries the importation of English dogs ceased, for the Germans were then in a position to use their own home-bred stock, and the breed was becoming increasingly popular. The Germans evolved two types, with markedly different characteristics in various parts of the country: the dogs which belonged to the north were heavily built, with strong chests and bold temperaments; those from the south were built on more elegant lines, and tended to be of a more nervous disposition.

There is surely no breed which has changed its name more often. In the sixteenth and seventeenth centuries Great Danes were mostly called English Dogge, but by 1680, when they were being bred in the German courts, the largest and best were called

Kammerhunde or Chamber Dogs, and were distinguished by the beautifully gilded and ornate collars which they wore. The second-best dogs wore collars with a silver finish, but at a later date they all became known as English Dogge. I feel this shows that the Germans considered them to be of English origin, although much later they adopted the Great Dane as the national breed of the fatherland.

Returning to earlier history, Dr. Morel MacKenzie in his book *Great Danes Past and Present* states 'as far as I can find out the Great Dane seems to have existed continuously from the earliest times in these Islands' (the British Isles).

Frederick Becker in his book *The Great Dane* (1905) says 'now it seems to me that the first specimens ever imported into England came from Denmark, and that from these old times the name "Great Dane" has been retained'.

In *The Great Dane*, by Virginia Keckler, she refers to Richard Blomes' engraving (1686) showing a boar hunt in Denmark. Thirteen hounds are pictured, most of which have cropped ears; from their size and general conformation one must conclude they are the breed we know today as the Great Dane. She says 'the colouring interested me particularly. Part of these are grey, some are spotted, and one appears to have the unusual spotting we have in Harlequins—black ears with one large spot on the shoulder.'

Early writers who mentioned and described these dogs for hundreds of years were Holinshed (1560), Camden (1568), Ware (1654) and Evelyn (1660–70).

Alexander Pope (1668–1744) owned perhaps the most famous of any Great Dane—a dog called Bounce who was his faithful companion for many years, and became well known through his master's writings. The Prince of Wales admired Bounce, and Pope later presented the Prince with a puppy.

Alexander Pope was notoriously cantankerous, and did not enjoy the best of health, but in spite of his stormy ravings he and Bounce were devoted to each other. Great Danes also seem to be excellent judges of character, and Bounce appeared no exception to this rule when his master hired a new valet whom he immediately disliked. On the first night of his employment the servant carried Pope to bed (the invalid being unable to do this for him-self), but Pope later awoke to see a man approaching the bed with a large knife. Unable to move, Pope screamed for his valet, but it was Bounce who dashed to the rescue and sprang on the intruder. The would-be killer turned out to be none other than the new valet, although it was never discovered why he intended to murder Pope.

As early as 1387, Gaston de Fois wrote his immortal *Luire du Chasse*: this was extremely well illustrated, and some of the dogs shown were Alaunts. There can be no doubt that these are Great Danes, the difference between them and Mastiffs being clearly defined.

Evelyn, writing between 1660 and 1670, described the Great Dane as 'a stately creature indeed, and did beat the cruel Mastiff'. There is thus little doubt that even then there was a clear dis-tinction between the two types of large dogs, although some writers have stated that there was at that time only the English Mastiff in these islands. Ray (1697) says 'it is the greatest dog I have ever seen', and Goldsmith (1770) says of the great Irish Wolfhound: 'I have seen about a dozen, the largest of these was about 4 ft. high. as tall as a calf at a year old. He was made extremely like a Greyhound, but more robust, and inclining to the figure of the French Matin or Great Dane.' Again, the acceptance of the Great Dane as a separate breed of dog is recognised.

Strabo writes of a large and powerful Greyhound in use among the Celtic and Pictic nations which was held in such high esteem by them as to have been imported into Gaul for the purposes of the chase. Dr. Morel MacKenzie says 'a picture is very much in my imagination, although exactly where I have seen it I cannot call to mind; it depicted a Viking in his ship under full sail, with a blue Great Dane standing in the bows'.

Constant appearances of a Great Dane in the paintings of Snyders, Rubens and Paulo Veronese leave little doubt as to the popularity of the breed in the Middle Ages.

A brace of large brindle dogs described as 'wild boar hounds' was presented to Her Royal Highness the Duchess of York in 1807. The delightful painting of this pair, Hannibal and Princess, shown with a litter of puppies, confirms that they were Great

Danes, although lacking the strength of head which we would expect to find today. Hannibal should not be confused with the famous Hannibal the Great, who was imported from Germany and was in fact born nearly a hundred years later.

Herr Otto Kreckwitz of Munich, a great authority on the breed, had no doubt about the Great Dane's antiquity, and said that 'the nearest approach to the German Dogge [the Great Dane] of our time is one that is represented on a Greek coin from Panormos, dating from the fifth century B.C. and now in the Royal Museum at Munich. This dog with cropped ears is exactly like a long-legged elegant Dogge, with a graceful neck.' Kreckwitz takes exception to the name Great Dane, on the grounds that the present form actually evolved in Germany, and should therefore be called German Dogge, in the same way as we in England have the Mastiff.

The breed changed its name many times, and Great Danes became known by different names in various parts of Germany, such as the *Ulm* Dog, or *Ulmer* Dog, Boar Hound, *Deutsche Dogge*, German Mastiff and Tiger Mastiff.

According to a letter written by Vere Shaw and published in *The Book of the Dog*, Herr Gustav Lang stated that all other names were to be abolished, and the breed should in future be known as German Mastiff. For some unspecified reason, however, the name German Mastiff was never adopted, and eventually the name *Deutsche Dogge* prevailed and remains today in Germany.

From *Modern Dogs*, by Rawdon Lee, published in 1906, we learn that the Great Dane was fast becoming a firm favourite in Britain. 'The ladies took him up, and the men patronised him, but the former could not always keep him in hand.' He also says 'handsome and symmetrical though he may be, he had always a temper and a disposition of his own, which could not be controlled when he became excited. Personally, I never considered the Great Dane suitable as a companion or domestic dog.'

It seems that at that time there was a rabies scare, and an order went out for all dogs to be muzzled and kept on a chain. This was a severe blow to the Great Dane; muzzling amazed him and made him savage—the restraint of the leash was not to be borne. He could not therefore be confined with safety, and such was the rabies problem that he had to be put down. As Rawdon Lee says, 'where once a dozen boar hounds reigned there is not one to be seen'.

The Great Dane today, however, is very different in temperament, and the dogs are famous for their trustworthy disposition and faithfulness to their owners.

The famous German statesman Prince Otto von Bismarck was well known for his admiration of the breed and owned several during his lifetime, one of which nearly caused an international incident by taking a dislike to a Russian diplomat! It seems that a somewhat spirited conversation was proceeding between the German Chancellor and the Russian Prime Minister, Gortschakoff. The latter was gesticulating rather more violently than usual, which led the dog Tyras, who lay on the rug, to suspect an attack on his master; springing at the proud Russian, he brought him to the floor! Apologies were profuse and accepted; Gortschakoff was not bitten, only frightened, and the peace of Europe remained undisturbed.

If another of Bismarck's Great Danes, Sultan, disliked a person he would take his judgement very much into account before making a decision. In *Modern Dogs*, Rawdon Lee says '. . . as a law student and official at Berlin, during his travels in many lands, throughout his diplomatic career at Frankfort, St. Petersburg, Paris and elsewhere, as well as at Varzin and at Friedrichsruh, Bismarck has always had the companionship of one or more of his favourite dogs. Probably the one to which he was most attached was Sultan, which died at Varzin in 1877'.

A writer in the *Kennel Gazette* gave the following interesting description of Prince Bismarck's favourite dog. I reproduce it here as illustrating the character and disposition of the ordinary Great Dane:

'Of all the dogs that have a place in history, Tyras, the noted Ulmer dog of the German Chancellor, is the only one whose death has been deemed of sufficient interest to be cabled round the world as an event, not merely of European, but of cosmopolitan interest. Indeed, the record of Tyras hardly ended with his life, for the cable has since told the world that the first visitor to Prince Bismarck on his recent birthday was the youthful emperor, who brought as a present another dog, of the type of the lamented Tyras. For nearly sixty years Prince Bismarck has owned specimens of the Great Dane, and generally has had one or more of unusual size. His first hound, acquired while living with his parents at Kniephof, was one of the largest ever seen, and was an object of awe to the peasantry of the district. This dog afterwards accompanied his young master to the college at Göttingen, where he speedily made his mark. Once when Bismarck was summoned to appear before the rector for throwing an empty bottle out of his window he took with him his enormous hound, to the great dismay of the reverend dignitary, who promptly found refuge behind a high-backed chair, where he remained until the hound had been sent out of the room. Bismarck was fined five thalers for bringing this "terrific beast" into the rector's sanctum, in addition to the punishment meted out for the original offence.'

Before the breed was officially named in Germany there was a variety referred to as the Tiger Dogge. In Germany 'Tiger' does not mean the colour of a tiger, but like a tiger horse (white with small dark spots) as opposed to a piebald horse, and possibly not unlike the Apaloosa or original Indian horse.

Herr Scheimeideberg gave the following description of the dog at this time:

'Figure high, elegant, head rather long; nose of medium length, thick, not pointed . . . point of nose large, black, except with Tiger dogs, where the same may be flesh coloured or spotted; lip trifle over-hanging, ears placed high and pointed, eyes brown, not too light (except with Tiger dogs, which often have glassy eyes); earnest and sharp look, neck pretty long and strong; without dewlap; chest broad and deep; back long and straight; toes closed, nails strong and long; thigh bone muscular; knees deep, almost like a Greyhound; tail not too long; hardly to reach the hocks and to be carried in a straight line with the back, never to be curly; the coat of the whole body, and particularly the tail, to be short and smooth; back dew claws are allowed on the hind feet if they are firm not loose; colour bright black, wavy, yellow, blue, if possible without any marks, or if striped usually with glassy eyes.'

The standard given out by Herr Scheimeideberg is probably the earliest drawn up in Germany. Most of the requirements could apply today, although the reference to colour as 'wavy 'is confusing, and it is hard to imagine what colour this would in fact be.

It seems that the British have always been criticised for crossing their colours, and another top German breeder of that period writes most emphatically about this:

'A very great fault in England of your breeders is to mix colours. . . . Harlequins *must* be black and white. We prefer the pure colours, but this does not seem to be the case in England.'

In *The Dog Encyclopedia* E. Malay Scott writes:

'Perfection of colour counts for much, but it can hardly be said to be an essential point . . . it influences neither soundness nor character and a Dane's best beauty can be obtained without it. Colour can be completed when form has begun.'

Hannibal the Great, born towards the end of the last century, was said to be one of the best Great Danes ever bred in Germany. His antecedents were shrouded in mystery, for he suddenly appeared on the market at Munich, and was immediately sold to a Mr. Ulrich for what was then a huge sum—£150. It is difficult to understand the lack of information about his breeding, for the Germans normally went to great pains to keep meticulous records of all their dogs. Although reported as being one of the best Danes ever seen, it appears that his colour was not good, though no details are available. If he was a bad colour this would explain his lack of pedigree, the Germans having always attached great importance to their colour breeding.

Hannibal the Great came to England but was not successful

as a stud dog. Unfortunately his short life came to a sad end when he was accidentally strangled in his kennel.

The Great Dane in Britain has had a rather chequered career. Firstly there was the near-extinction of the breed referred to by Rawdon Lee, when the rabies scare hit this country in the late nineteenth century. Then there was the expense of bringing stock in from Germany, which now had to go into quarantine for six months; fresh blood was thus limited, and the breed became severely inbred.

The situation seemed to be improving, with more and more enthusiasts for the Great Dane, when the breed was dealt yet another staggering blow. King Edward VII (then Prince of Wales) pronounced his dislike of cropping ears, and expressed a wish that the practice should cease. To lovers of the Great Dane at that time this was the last straw; the breed was once again threatened with extinction in this country, and for five or six years it was thought that the Dane would never regain its popularity in the British Isles.

Although it is generally thought that cropping in this country is now illegal, this is not so. King Edward's wishes never became law, though as far as all current breeders—and the Kennel Club—are concerned, the practice of cropping would be severely frowned upon. Were anyone to have a dog cropped here, the Kennel Club would not allow its progeny to be registered. This does not apply to imported cropped dogs, which cannot be entered for competition at dog shows, but may be entered at any show and benched provided they are listed 'Not for Competition'.

I can find no reference in Great Dane literature to the fact that the famous American Scout Colonel William Cody (later to be known the world over as Buffalo Bill) grew up with a Great Dane. In *The Last of the Great Scouts, Col. William Cody*, by Helen Cody Westmore (Colonel Cody's sister), she describes in great detail how as children they grew up with their beloved Great Dane called Turk. This dog seems to have had a profound influence upon the Cody children, for their Turk possessed sterling qualities which they greatly admired.

When as a young boy Buffalo Bill was describing his dog, he referred to him as 'an Ulm dog, Tiger Mastiff, German Boar

Hound, Great Dane. "Turk" is all of them put together.' Cody
was about ten years of age when Turk was bitten by a rabid dog.
This meant only one thing, and on a sad day, while young Bill
was out of earshot, it was arranged that the faithful Turk of the
Cody family should be shot. A sad little procession took Turk's
body high up east of Cody Hill, where he was given a funeral
service and buried. To mark the spot, Buffalo Bill found a large
block of red stone, which is common to that part of the country;
he squared it off, and wrote in large letters: 'Turk'.

When I was in Wyoming—the heart of the Buffalo Bill country
—I made enquiries about Buffalo Bill and Turk, and from his two
grandsons living in the town of Cody I ascertained that they had
heard talk of Turk. His grave on Cody Hill, Kansas, is lost, as
are the graves of Buffalo Bill's parents who were buried at the
same place. Perhaps one day someone will discover the piece of
rough-hewn stone which marks the place.

In later life Buffalo Bill became world famous and travelled to
Europe with his Wild West Show. Photographs are to be seen
showing the company with a Great Dane.

From Helen Cody Westmore's book *The Last of the Great
Scouts* I quote the following poem:

Burial of Turk

Only a dog! but the tears fall fast
As we lay him to rest underneath the green sod.
Where bountiful nature, the sweet summer through,
Will deck him with daisies and bright golden rod.

The loving thought of a boyish heart,
Marks the old dog's grave with a bloodstone red;
The name, carved in letters rough and rude,
Keeps his memory green, though his life be sped.

For the daring young hero of wood and plain,
Like all who are generous, strong and brave,
Has a heart that is loyal and kind and true,
And shames not to weep o'er his old friend's grave.

Only a dog, do you say? But I deem
A dog who with faithfulness fills his trust
More worthy than a man to be given
A tribute of love, when but ashes and dust.

One can see from this poem alone that Turk was an integral part of the Cody family, and his untimely and tragic death had a great impact upon them.

Many pens have retold the history of the Great Dane; with the passing of time little has been lost in the telling, and no doubt a certain amount of conjecture has been added. Most authorities are agreed, however, that dogs of great size have been portrayed and known for thousands of years, and at least one type of these immense dogs was neither as heavy in build as the Mastiff nor as light in structure as the Greyhound. In portraying the head of these dogs, artists have shown much of the Great Dane type. While it would seem foolish to say that a single breed has remained pure throughout the centuries, the types remain despite the mingling of blood-lines, and this gave earlier fanciers the opportunity to select and breed together the types they preferred and wanted to perpetuate.

2

The Early Great Dane

HAVING studied the early history of the breed we can now move on to the latter part of last century. This was the time when both English and German fanciers of the Great Dane became really absorbed in building this handsome dog into the most striking member of the canine race, the 'Apollo of all breeds'.

It has very often been said that the Great Dane is a German dog, but I am unable to agree with this view. History does not establish in any way that the breed is native to Germany, or indeed to any other country in the world. However, full credit must be given to the Germans for having 'made' the breed as we know it today; the early German breeders undoubtedly drew up the master plan, and set the high standard which has varied little over the years. Due to their tenacity of purpose and high-class selective breeding they quickly evolved a large, strong, symmetrical dog of great beauty.

After the war of 1870, when Germany was filled with martial ardour and patriotism, it seemed appropriate to choose a national dog for the Fatherland; they selected the big, powerful variety which was already well known to them, and christened him the *Deutsche Dogge*. In those days any owner tended to think that his was the correct type, but it was only by the interchange of stock and ideas between various cities, careful consideration of the good and bad points of different dogs, special attention to finer details (e.g. texture of coat, quality of head), and constant culling of unsuitable specimens, that the Germans finally fixed on a definite type which they considered to be satisfactory.

The tremendous strides which have been made can be fully appreciated when one sees a picture of Rolf I, a big German winner of 1883, and compares him with our best modern specimens. However, his famous sire, Nero owned by Herr E. Messter and winner of the Prix d'Honneur at Berlin in 1878, Hanover in 1879 and Elderfield in 1880, must have been well ahead of his time for both type and size. Pictures show us a noble, impressive animal, standing four square; given a little more length of fore-face, he could take his place amongst the best champions today.

The first German dog show took place in 1863 at Hamburg, and we are told that 'some very grave-looking doggen took part in the event'. Of these 'grave-looking doggen', eight were called *Danish Doggen* and seven were referred to as *Ulmer Doggen*. The Czar of Russia purchased two of them.

The next recorded exhibition was held in 1869 at Hamburg-Altona, when fifteen *Danish Doggen* and twelve *Ulmer Doggen* were apparently shown. Then in 1876, at the Great Dane Dog Show in Hamburg, there were twenty-four *Danish Doggen* and forty-five *Ulmer Doggen*. It would appear that the breed was now really catching on, for it would be a sizable dog show anywhere in the world today which could attract nearly seventy individual Great Danes, yet these were still the early days of the breed as a show animal and as the new national dog of Germany.

The name 'Danish Doggen'—at first more popular than 'German Doggen'—was rapidly losing ground, for none had seen Denmark, nor had any of them even been born there, as their pedigree papers indicated. In the main these large dogs belonged to the citizens of Hamburg, although some had been bred in Berlin and partly in Württemberg, South Germany.

At that time (1876) a group of show judges declared that it was impossible to separate the two breeds *Danish Doggen* and *Ulmer Doggen*, for they were in fact one and the same. They further suggested that in future all these dogs should be known as *Deutsche Doggen*.

There was at first some difficulty in making the name *Deutsche Doggen* prevail, and different names were continually being used until the dog show held at Hanover in 1879. Many breeders met there, and decided to call the heavier Danes *Danish Doggen* and the lighter weight Danes *Ulmer Doggen*—so they appeared to be back where they started! In spite of this decision, brindle Danes were often called *Hatzrüden* or Wolf Dogs, while the fawn-coloured and sometimes the blue Danes were called *Danish Doggen*, regardless of weight or size. I find this rather interesting, because it appears that even then, there was still a very strong feeling that the breed had certain connections with Denmark, and finally to drop the name Danish seemed a very hard thing to do.

At this particular time harlequin Great Danes were bred mainly in South Germany, whilst the breeders in North Germany preferred to breed blue dogs. In later years this position was reversed, and there were far more harlequin kennels to be found in the north.

The year 1880 finally brought acceptance of the official new name for the Great Dane, and from that time he has been known in Germany as the *Deutsche Dogge*. Breed fanciers throughout the world like to refer to him as the 'Apollo of the Dog World', a noble and charming title but quite unofficial.

In France, however, the Great Dane is still known as the *Grand Danois*, while in England in 1892 he was referred to as the German Mastiff. This is hard to understand, for at an earlier date still he was, in fact, known as the English Dogge. In Denmark he was called the Great Danish Dog. This naturally caused much confusion from time to time, although we are told that it was the French naturalist Buffon who first used the name *Grand Danois*, or Great Dane, in France, remarking at the same time that under the influence of the Danish climate the Greyhound had become the *Grand Danois*! A remark which could well have been made with tongue in cheek.

In those days the big 'yellow dogs' lacked black masks and points, these not being considered at all desirable 'for they were indicative of a Mastiff cross'. One might surmise that the name arose because like the Danish people they were tall and fair; in other words, the 'big blonde dogs' could quite easily have become the *Grand Danois* or the Great Dane, and this could account for the inability of past historians to establish a definite connection between the Great Dane and Denmark.

In 1874 a new era began when the famous German breeder, Herr Max Hartenstein, bought a Great Dane at Stuttgart. This dog was called Württembergischer Hatzrude (known as Bosco), and after the purchase of a bitch named Bella in 1876, Herr Hartenstein bred many Great Danes until 1895, and showed many excellent specimens. He did not hesitate to buy the best breeding material regardless of cost, and so began an illustrious course for the whole breed at that time, especially in Germany.

Hartenstein's most famous dogs were Faust I and his three daughters Goldperl, Otter and Schwalbe. His best black Great Danes were Peter, Cora II, Sandor II and Nigra; the best of the blues were Faust I, Faust II, Faust III, Thibo, Falkner-Plavia, Prima, Perle v. Plaven, Schwalbe, Otter, Maximus and Flora Plavia. His best brindles were Rex, Mustapha, Stella, Ilka II, Armida, Girofla, Goldperl, Ruth, Bella Vista, Venus v. Plaven and Primas. Ilka II was sold to England for 1,500 marks. The best of his harlequins were Bravo (porcelain tiger), Dorina, Milo (dark blue harlequin) and Dora, and the best yellow Danes were Bosca, Electra, Mora, Bacchus and Sandor.

Then in 1873 Herr Messter, a breeder in North Germany, started a kennel of Great Danes; many of these, and those of Herr Hartenstein, appear in the pedigrees recorded in the early *Deutsche Doggen Club* Stud Books. His greatest triumphs were in the years between 1880 and 1890, and from the records it appears that he took the breed and shows by storm. In Berlin in 1880 he had thirty-two Great Danes entered, and in 1881, 1883, and 1885 he exhibited in London, on each occasion showing twenty dogs. Then in Russia at the St. Petersburg Show in 1887 he exhibited twenty-two Great Danes.

Herr Messter's best dogs were Nero I, Nero II, Sultan I, Sultan II, Mentor I, Pluto, Apollo, Cedric, Tiger, Cyrus I, Cyrus II, Brutus, Bella I, Bella II, Minka I, Minka II, Euphrat, Viola, Vineta, Juno, Zampa II, Ceras, Judith and Tyra.

Herr B. Ulrich was another successful breeder from South Germany who produced many good Great Danes over a long period of time, and had many of the best specimens. His outstanding period was between 1882 and 1887, and several of his dogs proved to have a great influence on the breed. Harras II, his sons Corvin, Harras III, Helios, Hannibal, Halfdan and Hermes were particularly famous, whilst his best bitches were

Diane Pearce

Ch. Fergus of Clausentum

Thomas Fall

Ch. Rebeller of Ouborough

Nero

Merle Great Dane. Painting by Maud Earl

Lord Topper. From the original by R. H. Moore, 1900

Ch. Hannibal of Redgrave. From the original by R. H. Moore, 1907

Fauna Moguntia,
Ch. Dolf v.d. Saal-
burg and Ch. Bosko
v.d. Saalburg
Dauer

Ch. Dolf v.d. Saal-
burg   *Dauer*

Ger. and Am. Ch.
Etfa v.d. Saalburg

Nora-Doos, Bella II (which one assumes he purchased from Herr Messter), Ilka, Senta, Noritta and Noriega.

Another large and important kennel at that time was owned by the well-known Herr E. Aichele of Berlin in 1886. He specialised in the blue variety, and bred and showed his dogs under the kennel name of Schwalbennest. The most famous were Falkner I and his son Talisman v. Schwalbennest, and in bitches he owned such famous blues as Blaue Donau, Iris and the outstanding specimen Vesta. He bought Blaue Donau in 1902 at Vienna, and Iris and Vesta were sisters born of Otter I (Faust Hartenstein and Flora) and Falkner I.

Other famous breeders of that era were Prinz Zu Solms, Dr. Bodinus, Dr. Caster, and Herr Burger, Herr Essig and Herr Cohn.

Milo Denlinger tells in his book *The Complete Great Dane* how the second International Dog Show took place at Hanover in 1882. A complete record of this event is available, and he describes the details:

'It is interesting to note in the judges' report how many Great Danes were there, and that a single breeder had twenty-two entries. The principal faults noted in the show dogs were too much dewlap, too strong lips, and pointed muzzles. About half of the sixty-five Great Danes were rated very good, as was frequently the case in those years at the end of the century, and some tiger dogs were mentioned as being of especial interest.'

It is recorded that it was very difficult for breeders of Danes to get a proper position assigned to them between the *Bullenbiesen* and the Greyhound. The *Dog Magazine* of 1882 states:

'Sometimes Great Danes are entered as *Ulmer Doggen*, Danish Dogs or *Hatzrüden*, but everyone who is at least informed is aware that only the name *Deutsche Dogge* is correct. In recent shows the St. Bernards and Newfoundlands did not make a good impression, but the Great Danes were uniformly good in coat colour and conformation of their bodies. It is a pity that we so seldom have English Doggen (Mastiffs) shown here. When we think of the great shows in England, when eighty to a hundred Mastiffs, all of great weight, may be seen at one Show, we realise what an excellent appearance our elegant *Deutsche Dogge* would present by way of contrast.'

A concluding remark states that a fancier paid 500 thaler for one of the Great Danes which had been exhibited.

An important show took place in Stuttgart in 1887, when more than 300 Great Danes were entered. As far as is known, this is the largest number of individual specimens entered for any one show. Many other shows with huge entries occurred in Germany: for example, the Berlin Show held in 1888 had 108 dogs, at the Frankfurt/Main Show in the same year 110 Great Danes made up the entry. Then, in 1889, 116 Great Danes were shown in Cologne, and Herr Hartenstein's Neckar, Otter and Ruth all took first prizes in the show at Kassel. In the autumn of that year a dog show was held at Cannstadt, Württemberg, when Hannibal received a prize given by His Royal Majesty King Karl.

From information we have on German show Danes of this period it appears that one of the most important Great Danes between 1885 and 1893 was the brindle Harras I, owned by Dr. Caster and grandsire of Hannibal. He was said not to be unusual in height or of a good colour, but he had such a wonderful body that he always took the first prize after the judges had observed him carefully. Equally important was Harras II, whose owner, Herr Ulrich of Doos, was the winner of prizes at Vienna, Munich and Leipzig in 1886.

We also read of a very beautiful lightweight bitch, with a slim body; she was shown at Munich in 1886, and caused quite a sensation because of the coquettish way she carried her head and her general bearing. Her colouring, too, was unusual, since she was white with yellow and brown spots.

Hannibal I was considered to be one of the best Great Danes of all time. Originally owned by Herr Ulrich, details of his later life are rather vague. Rawdon Lee states that he was purchased for a large sum of money by a Mr. Wilby of England, and describes him as 'an enormous dog of immense power, but perhaps a little heavier and too Mastiff like to quite please some of our [British] insular prejudices'. Then he tells us of Hannibal I's sad end, and how he was found hung in his kennel.

In *The Complete Great Dane*, Milo Denlinger says:

> 'Hannibal I was a very good brindle male owned by B. Ulrich. His sire was Moreau (Dr. Caster's Harras I from Hartnicks Liza) and his dam was Flora, born in 1887. Hannibal I was probably one of the best Great Danes of his time in Germany. He was sold in 1892 for a high price to England, and from there was sold to Moscow.'

As you can see, records regarding Hannibal after he left Germany are not as clear as we would wish, and Denlinger's and Malay Scott's accounts do not completely agree.

In 1888 the *Deutsche Doggen Club* was formed, and about 1892 the *official* breed standard was published, probably for the first time, although Herr Scheimeideberg had previously issued an excellent description (see Chapter 1) which was probably used as a basis for the standard finally drawn up by the *Deutsche Doggen Club*.

Undoubtedly German stock was in demand the world over, and many famous dogs were exported to England, America, France and the Netherlands. Prior to the outbreak of the First World War, Germany had achieved supremacy in the breeding of Great Danes.

Now to look at the earlier fanciers in England. The Great Dane Club was formed in 1883—five years before the *Deutsche Doggen Club* came into existence—and it seems that from early days breeders were just as keen in both countries, also in America. However, I feel that Germany's idea of adopting the handsome Great Dane as symbolic of her own feeling of greatness gave them the incentive to forge ahead in perfecting this marvellous and noble breed of dog. In this country breeders had a far more personal attitude—which unfortunately still exists today in many cases—over breeding Great Danes.

Adcock was a name closely associated with Great Danes at this time, and he was one of the earliest exhibitors in England. He had a number of animals which made a name for themselves in more ways than one! Showing in Lancashire he then had the celebrated dog Satan, which got at loggerheads with a Newfoundland; the latter, according to eyewitness reports, 'poor thing, was shaken like a rat, and would have soon ceased to live, excepting in memory, had not three stout men choked off the immense German dog'.

Satan, however, must take a leading place in the early introduction—or rather re-introduction—of the breed into the British Isles. We are told that his temper was 'so bad', and that he was a dark-coloured dog, with strong head and jaw, that would not be at all popular with present-day admirers of the Dane. However, his owner, Mr. Adcock, must be given full credit, for he was one of the greatest fanciers of the time, and through his patronage the Great Dane Club was established. Another famous dog of his was the richly coloured brindle Ivanhoe, who repeatedly won prizes at the leading shows.

It was not until a year after the formation of the Great Dane Club that classes were first provided for the breed at Birmingham in 1884, the Kennel Club having acknowledged them as a recognised breed in their Stud Book of that year.

During 1863–4 Sir Richard Palmer was said to have owned a big white and black dog which was 35 in. at the shoulder, 200 lb in weight, and was a Great Dane! Rawdon Lee says:

'I never saw a dog of this variety approaching this size, and at that time a 200 lb weight dog had not been produced. Satan himself, a very heavy dog, would not be more than perhaps one hundred and fifty pounds at the most.'

Later, in June 1885, a dog show devoted entirely to Great Danes was held at Ranelagh Club grounds, Mr. Gambier Bolton being the judge. This was just the time when the breed was reaching the height of its popularity here, and the sixty dogs made a wonderful show, benched under the lime trees in these historic grounds. Never before had such a gathering of these magnificent dogs been seen in this country, among them the great fawn dog Cedric the Saxon, perfect in symmetry. With Captain Graham, the noted Irish Wolfhound authority, Rawdon Lee carefully measured Cedric, who stood 33¼ in. at the shoulder. The two experts then took the height of several of the biggest animals present, and found it 'was extraordinary how 35 in. and 36 in. animals dwindled down, some of them nearly ½ in. at a time!' People change little with the passing of time, and I feel even today that some dogs claimed to be a certain height have been measured with over-enthusiasm by their owners.

Other tall dogs exhibited at Ranelagh were Herbert Leal, who stood 33¾ in. at the shoulders and weighed 182 lb, and Mr. Riego's brindle dog Cid Campeador, who stood exactly 33½ in. and weighed 175 lb.

Quoting again from Rawdon Lee, he says that:

'This couple were the tallest of their race I have seen up to that time, but, at Brighton Show in 1895 I weighed and measured a dog called Morro, the property of Mr. Woodruffe Hill. He stood fully 34 in. at the shoulder and scaled 190 lb.'

Great Danes were now now being classified at all the important shows and were steadily gaining in popularity. Mr. Gambier Bolton, who officiated at the very first specialist show, organised by the Great Dane Club, must have been at that time one of the foremost authorities on the breed in this country. As secretary of the newly formed club, it was he who first drew up the standard of the breed—which one imagines was subsequently fully approved by the committee of the club. On what he based his standards it is hard to know, for the official breed standard of the *Deutsche Doggen Club* was not to be published for a further nine years! One would assume, however, that as the German and English standards are basically the same, both were founded on Herr Scheimeiderberg's excellent description, which is the earliest-known detailed blueprint of the breed.

Although in the Great Dane Club Book dated 1890 we find the following information:

'Under the title of Great Dane Club are included the various differently coloured specimens known as German Mastiffs,

Tiger Mastiffs, and Boarhounds. It would be interesting to know whether these three "breeds" were all different colours. The standard for judging was in accord with that fixed by the principal clubs and breeders abroad—at a meeting held in Berlin 1880.'

Again, the dates seem confusing and mysterious. The *Deutsche Doggen Club* was not in existence before 1880, and we have no record of earlier 'breed clubs' in Germany. I think we may safely assume that at the meeting held at the Berlin Show in 1880 the nucleus of the standard (since taken and used the world over) was drafted by a gathering of knowledgeable, enthusiastic and highly successful German breeders.

Returning to Mr. Gambier Bolton's first standard, the most interesting part is the reference to colour. It appeared that anything would do, and even from the earliest time of show Danes in this country it seemed that the Germans were justified in their accusations that we attached little importance to colour, no mention being made of harlequins. However, at a general meeting held later in October 1905 a new resolution was carried regarding colour.

Our Friend the Dog, by Dr. Gordon Stables, R.N., gives the whole of the first standard as drawn up by Gambier Bolton. Since the general part varies very little from the present standard, I quote only on colour and markings:

'The recognised colours are, the various shades of Grey (commonly called Blue), Red, Black, or pure White, or White with patches of the beforementioned colours.

These colours are sometimes accompanied with markings of a darker tint about the eyes and muzzle, and with a line of the same tint (called a trace) along the course of the spine.

The above ground colours also appear in Brindles, and are also the ground colours of the mottled specimens.

The mottled specimens have irregular patches, or clouds, upon the above-named ground colours; in some instances the clouds or markings being of two or more tints.

In the mottled specimens the wall or china eye is not uncommon, and the nose often parti-coloured or wholly flesh coloured.

In the whole-coloured specimens the china eye but rarely appears, and the nose more or less approaches black, according to the prevailing tint of the dog, and the eyes vary also in colour.

The whole-coloured reddish yellow, with black muzzle and ears, is the colour least cared for, as it is indicative of the Mastiff cross.'

It is obvious from the above that Gambier Bolton had made a close study of the breed, and was fully acquainted with the finer points and characteristics which are still associated with the various colours.

It seems likely that the 'mottled specimens' referred to would be the Merles, no longer accepted as a show colour, and possibly the harlequins which come from the same family. White Danes were also acceptable, but one wonders how often they appeared, for I have never seen a picture of one, nor heard of anyone who has bred pure white animals. Again, the red fawn with the black mask was the least desirable, for it gave evidence of Mastiff crossing; a very different story from today, for this colour is now one of the most sought after and highly prized, particularly in the United States.

With the ever-rising cost of living it is surprising to find that the annual subscription of the Great Dane Club in 1883 was two guineas, plus a further two guineas entrance fee! This was a small fortune in those days, and it is difficult to appreciate how, in our present affluent society, the annual subscription should have been reduced to one guinea when everything else has increased tenfold.

Another famous English breeder was Mr. Schmidt of Hackney, London, best known for his renowned Lord Topper, who was a great winner in the 1890s and said to be 'one of the largest and strongest and most active dogs living. He is a capital stock getter.' Mr. Schmidt had many other notable dogs, but it was Lord Topper who was most prized and had a great influence on the breed.

Mr. R. Leadbetter, of Buckinghamshire, kept a kennel of about thirty animals and was a name associated with some of the best Great Danes. His most famous dog was probably the beautifully marked harlequin The Czar, said to have 'coal black markings on a white ground'. He was purchased by Mr. Leadbetter from a Parisian dealer, M. Aaron, in October 1897, and arrived in England with a brilliant continental show record which he fully maintained here.

Another famous dog belonging to Mr. Leadbetter was also imported—a fawn called Ch. Count Fritz who was whelped on the 29th June 1890. Bred in Germany by Herr Carl Kesberg, he was by Cyrus ex Storma, both of whom were big winners at the continental shows. Ch. Count Fritz, when he appeared at the English show, was said 'to excel in body, legs and feet, possessing also substance with quality, and being a capital mover'.

Mr. J. Everett's King Oscar was also a top-class Dane of that period, although 'owing to a slight accident to a hind leg was not much exhibited, but has won well at Chelmsford, Nottingham and Leicester'. He was offered at stud for the magnificent fee of three guineas!

Mr. Boyes, of Bolton, Lancashire, imported some very fine specimens from Germany, and had much success with his de Grace Danes, although he was not the most active of exhibitors. Like so many breeders of that day and age, he had more than his share of bad luck, and the loss of his famous dog Leo de Grace was a great blow which spurred him to look on the Continent for another dog closely resembling Leo. From Germany he bought a very good dog which was shown in this country under the name Tyrus de Grace; said to be 'a light fawn', but an excellent specimen of the breed, excelling in head, neck and shoulders, and 'we know none with a better front'.

The breed had now got off to a flying start in England, but was soon to receive a severe blow. On 27th February 1895 the Kennel Club passed a regulation which forbade cropping and stated that after 1901 no cropped dogs could be shown. This was instigated by King Edward VII (then Prince of Wales) who—as stated in the previous chapter—had expressed a wish that the cropping of dogs should be banned.

It can be understood how breeders felt about this, and in fact so strong was the feeling that the Great Dane would lose his whole character because of the new rule that scarcely one remained in the fancy. Before the year was out a meeting was held by Mr. Hood-Wright at the 1895 Cruft's, attended by a dozen or so enthusiasts and also by Dr. Morel MacKenzie, later to become an accepted authority on the breed. The Great Dane Club was re-formed, with Mr. Hood-Wright elected as the honorary secretary, and in the Club Book issued in 1896 the following were given as the officers and committee:

President: Mr. R. Leadbetter
Hon. Treasurer: Mr. R. Miller
Hon. Secretary: Mr. R. Hood-Wright
Committee: Messrs. Morley, Allanson, J. Baehr, E. N. N. Bartlett, E. R. Clemmens, R. Cook, E. E. Fox, R. Head, Hales Parry, S. Pendry, C. Petrywalski, J. Trainor and J. Transel

Mr. Hood-Wright held the post of hon. secretary until 1903, when he left to settle in Ceylon; his place was then taken by Dr. Morell MacKenzie, who was secretary for a number of years.

Today 'dogdom' is very much a woman's world, nearly 90 per cent of the exhibitors and breeders being female. It is interesting to note that all the 1898 executive and committee were male.

One of the most important periods in the history of the breed was in the years from 1895 to 1905, when Mrs. Violet Horsfall of Norfolk bred the famous Redgraves Great Danes. She became 'the queen of Great Danes'. Founding her line on Nero and other famous German dogs, she produced the finest specimens yet seen and became founder of the modern Great Dane in this country.

Rawdon Lee, who was a writer at that time, knew the Great Dane and his enthusiasts well, was closely associated with the breeders and knew many of the dogs personally. He says:

'. . . perhaps the best all-round Great Dane we have had here was the brindled bitch Vendetta of Redgrave . . . she was not particularly a big bitch, though perhaps taller and heavier than she looked by reason of her symmetry. She stood $31\frac{1}{2}$ in. at the shoulder and weighed 140 lb; but in general form and correctness of type of head, without lippiness or hound-like appearance, she was pretty nearly perfect.'

Ch. Vendetta was bred in Germany and was by the illustrious Harras ex the equally illustrious Flora.

There were many other famous Redgraves, Ch. Viceroy, Ch. Thor, Ch. Vlrest, Ch. Viola, to mention a few which had a profound impact on the breed. One of the most important and memorable events occurred when Ch. Hannibal of Redgrave beat the 'crack' German Ch. Bosco Colonia, whose owner Herr Dobleman had brought him over with great confidence to endeavour to beat all comers. The early breeders certainly had more thrills in the show ring than we experience today.

Mrs. Spark, of Sawbridgeworth, Hertfordshire, had several famous harlequins, one of her best being Superba of Stapleton. The Redgrave and Stapleton kennels usually monopolised the chief prizes at the shows.

In 1905 Mrs. Horsfall began to take less interest in the showing and breeding of Great Danes, but during the ten years that she was actively concerned she had attained a pinnacle of fame never before equalled in this country, and unlikely to be surpassed in the future. She undoubtedly established English Great Danes as we know them now, and today there is unlikely to be a fawn or brindle Great Dane which does not stem from the illustrious Redgraves. Mrs. Horsfall retired at her zenith—a decision few people are wise enough to make in any field of activity. As a famous handler once said after winning Best in Show at the Westminster Show (America's most important dog show), 'When you have reached the top of the mountain, there is nowhere else to go, but down!' How right he was. So it was with Mrs. Horsfall, for she left the breed when she was at the height of her success.

America, too, had just as early an interest in the Great Dane as Germany and England, and the first recorded Great Dane in the States was a male called Prince, belonging to Mr. Francis Butler of New York, in 1857. Prince was said to be in a class of his own, and quite probably came from Germany. However, he must have been an extraordinary dog, and during a visit to England was presented to Her Majesty Queen Victoria. In 1891 a German dog called Imperator was sold to a Chicago fancier, being advertised as 'the largest dog in the world'. Imperator was placed at stud at a fee of twenty guineas—an enormous sum of money in those days!

At an American show held in 1881 it was apparently said that 'the Danes were such a bad-tempered lot'; Mr. Lincoln, then acting as the show superintendent of the New York Show, went out of his way to have the breed banned. However, in spite of all this, Great Danes continued to make headway in the United States, and in 1890 two classes put on for the breed attracted twenty-five dogs and nine bitches. In 1905 it was said that the Americans 'had more good Great Danes than any other breed', and the New York Show of that year had the wonderful entry of seventy-seven Danes.

It was in 1889 that the American Speciality Club was founded, later to be known—as it still is today—as the Great Dane Club of America. By this time the Americans had drawn up their standard, which was based closely on the German requirements. A prominent writer of the day, James Watson, in *The Dogbook* published in 1906, says that the 'American standard regarding the mouth is to be preferred to that of the English'.

Up to the year 1900 there were fourteen recorded champions in America, and it is interesting to note that only one of these was fawn, two were harlequins, and the remaining eleven were brindles. America, like England, continued to improve the breed, and many imports from Germany came into both countries. Because of her size, however, and the fact that she has never had quarantine restrictions, America has always been able to import from Germany on a far greater scale than England.

In those early days breeders were beset by many hazards completely unknown today, so that one wonders how such progress was made in the face of so many difficulties. Although good food was accepted as a 'must' for the growing youngsters, the importance of vitamins, etc., was not realised as it is today. Many bitches died whelping, and Caesarians were practically unknown. Science had not then discovered how to prevent and cure many diseases and illnesses. Losses through distemper were colossal, and one wonders how the breeders overcame such heartbreaks, and were not too discouraged to continue.

Herr Messter of Berlin, one of the earliest breeders and owner of Nero, says that he suffered heavy losses due to distemper, abortion and so on. During 1881 he lost forty young Great Danes through distemper in two weeks; after the Hanover Show in 1882 he lost a further fourteen adults. He felt that the breed's short coat made it more sensitive than others; while this would not, of course, be our view today, they were battling then with a disease which baffled them, and during the course of time Herr Messter lost hundreds of puppies.

Another famous breeder of Berlin, Herr Kirschbaum, makes some interesting comments which still hold good:

'It is not desirable to let the Dane take too long walks, during his first eight months. He needs a good place to play, but if one takes long walks, the bones and sinews will not develop properly. Even with the best care, the young Dane does not present a very good appearance to his owner as he is growing up. From the age of five months until he is a year old, one can see many faults in him. For example, the head does not look Dane-like, the body is clumsy, and there are no signs of elegance.

At one period, the dog looks too high in front, and at another time the hind-quarters seem to be much higher. The legs seem bad, and the splay feet are dreadful. Suddenly the dog carries his tail poorly, and his hair seems too coarse, etc. But all these faults will vanish in most cases by the time the Dane is two years old, so his owner should not be too troubled about him.'

Those breeders of a century ago had some of the rearing worries we still experience—particularly with the very big puppy which can sometimes almost outgrow his strength.

A problem which all the early breed stalwarts had in common was the uncertain temperament of the Great Dane, for he was not considered entirely trustworthy. The Germans have often aimed to produce a 'mean' streak. I feel this is because—as with so many of their breeds including the Great Dane—they have bred primarily for guard-dog and watchdog instincts. The British and Americans have always required more kindly dispositions in all their breeds, and it is to their credit that they make equable temperament a paramount feature.

In conclusion I feel it is right that we should acknowledge the debt we owe to those breeders of an earlier era, for it is through their indomitable spirit and true love of the breed that fanciers of today are able to enjoy this most wonderful creature—the Great Dane.

3

Great Danes between the Wars

THE years between the First and Second World Wars can only be described as golden years for Great Danes. Germany, having already bred to a high standard of excellence, continued to breed still greater dogs. England entered into a new era, developing the breed to a high level of quality, while in America, too, interest was just as keen.

Germany had always been most fortunate in that her pioneer breeders were dedicated people whose one aim was to produce splendid *Deutsche Doggen* for the fatherland. Personal interest did not overlay national interest, which I feel was a major factor in their success, for the rapid improvement of the Great Dane in Germany, which could fairly be called the land of its development, was meteoric indeed.

Between the wars, and even prior to the First World War, fanciers were in the main people with a vast experience of live-stock; often closely connected with horses or cattle, they had an innate knowledge of and aptitude for breeding dogs. For want of a better expression, they were oft-times called 'stockmen'—people with a natural flair for breeding good stock, whether it be horses or pigeons.

Over the years we have seen many social changes—some for the better. Nowadays, however, a different type of person is attracted to dog breeding, and as a well-known person in this sphere said to me only recently, 'they are not dog people, in the accepted sense'. A few, fortunately, are willing to learn, but the vast majority are carried away by an excellent head, or a dog that shows like a dream; they fail to see the unsightly steep croups, straight shoulders, flat ribs and other structural defects which would have immediately offended the eye of our old-timers.

Commercialisation had not reared its head in the dog world in the earlier days, and those who bred Great Danes did so because they loved the breed and passionately wanted to see it progress. Therefore, at this time in their history, a happy state of affairs existed—I have purposely refrained from saying 'ideal' state of affairs, for although the circumstances were far better than today, I am quite sure they were not perfect. On the other hand, there were experienced 'animal people' who knew the correct make, shape and balance, and knew also that without these basic requirements no animal can be really great.

Again, there were wealthy people willing to sink vast sums into their interest and hobby. Some thought this was not good for the breed, but I feel they were short-sighted in their outlook, for where the best stock in the world can be imported into a country regardless of cost this can do nothing but good for a breed and its future.

In England the next greatest era after the Redgrave Danes was when Mr. J. V. Rank and Mr. Gordon Stewart became interested in the breed. Both were millionaires, and were prepared to spend large fortunes on bringing into the country some of the finest specimens in the world—most of which at that time were to be found in Germany. From 1921 until 1936 Mr. Rank imported no fewer than twenty-five Great Danes, while Mr. Stewart imported fifty-five specimens between 1926 and 1936. Between the two wars eighty-six Great Danes in all were imported into England, so one can imagine the amount of excellent foreign stock which was available for breeders to choose from when selecting a stud dog.

It was during these years that such illustrious dogs as Ch. Pampa of Ouborough, Ch. Primley Pericles, Ch. Vivien of Ouborough, Ch. Bellovien of Ouborough, Ch. Rebeller of Ouborough, Ch. Raider of Ouborough, Ch. Ruffian of Ouborough and many others made their mark, not only for Mr. Rank and his Ouborough kennels, but also for Great Danes in England.

Mr. Gordon Stewart, with Ch. Egmund of Send, Ch. Lancelot of Send, Ch. Midas of Send (owned by His Royal Highness Prince George, Duke of Kent), Ch. Vlana of Send, Ch. Rahie of Send,

Ch. Danilo of Send, etc., also contributed much towards the history of the breed. There are few Great Danes in this country today which do not go back to the Send or Ouborough breeding, and many Danes stem directly from both these lines.

At this time the Kennel Club allowed 'change of name', which is fortunately no longer permitted. However, it did allow exhibitors to re-register a dog with a completely different name from that first recorded by the breeder. There were thus many imported dogs which were promptly re-registered by their new owners on arrival here. Also, when famous dogs changed hands in this country they were frequently exhibited under a new name incorporating the kennel name of the latest owner. Some famous dogs did retain their original name, but these were in the minority. I feel this was a great pity, for a dog could thus become 'lost' in the pedigree of the future.

One of the most important newcomers to England after the First World War was the brindle dog Valthari of Bellary; imported in 1921 by Miss Callinder, now Mrs. Elliott, this dog was unbeaten in the show ring in Germany. Mrs. Elliott, who now lives in Surrey and no longer owns any Danes, told me that when she brought this grand dog into the country nearly fifty years ago he was 'not for sale out of Germany', and the only way she was able to procure him was to have a friend purchase him on her behalf.

In 1921, also, Mr. Rank imported five dogs, and in 1923 he brought four more into the country. In 1926 he acquired Ziska v. Zobtenburg, which, while in quarantine, had a litter to Rex Landor v. Zeltnerschloss.

However, it was not until 1926 that Mr. Gordon Stewart—who was also to make a sensational name with his 'Send' Great Danes —first imported, bringing in no fewer than twenty-five new specimens!

Both these kennels were producing first-class animals, and teams were regularly shown from both the Send and Ouborough strongholds, vying with each other in the show ring for the plum prizes. Although Mr. Rank kept a large kennel which was capably managed by Mr. W. G. Siggers, it was Mr. Gordon Stewart who went in for keeping huge numbers of dogs in his Send kennels, which were said to be 'one of the biggest breeding establishments in the world', at one time reputedly housing several hundred adults. Mr. Stewart was very keen on obedience and on training generally; his dogs were well schooled and gave many clever displays which became famous throughout the country. Many of the Send Danes were trained to a high standard of perfection, and were frequently matched successfully against Alsatians to test their brain power.

In 1921 Mr. Siggers, who was to successfully manage the Ouborough kennels throughout its entire career, had a bitch called Viola. She was bred out of the famous and illustrious Rufflyn line of Mr. Coates, which produced a number of champions before the outbreak of the First World War, and also in the early twenties. In 1922 Viola was transferred to Mr. Rank, re-registered as Lisa of Ouborough and won Kennel Club Challenge Certificates for her new owner under this name.

Mr. Rank's interest was originally with harlequins, and some of his earliest Danes were Ch. Magpie of Etive and Ch. Marcus of Walsall.

One of the most famous dogs was Ch. Primley Pericles, born in 1923 and bred by Mr. Whitney, who under the prefix of 'Primley' had many notable animals. Purchased by Mr. Rank in 1925, Ch. Pericles' most famous offspring was the lovely Ch. Vivien of Ouborough, and from the same litter came Ch. Pibe of Ouborough. An interesting thing about Pericles was that he was not shown until 1927, when he had a brilliant show career and quickly attained his title.

The import race continued between these two great kennels, and in 1927 Mr. Rank imported five new Great Danes while Mr. Stewart added a further six. In 1928 they each brought six new specimens into the country! Then in 1929–30 only Mr. Stewart imported, bringing in a further five animals; it was not until 1931 that Mr. Rank decided to add more new stock to his Ouborough kennels, and brought in six Danes, with Mr. Stewart still keeping up his numbers.

It would appear that both these great kennels were achieving what they wanted, and had now developed their own strains, for the number of dogs being imported by Send and Ouborough had rapidly declined. In fact, in 1932 Mrs. Butt and Miss Startin were the only breeders to bring in fresh blood. Mr. Rank imported two more in 1935, and the following year Mrs. Lee Booker and Mrs. Bhanubandh were the only people to import two animals.

Returning to the top kennels of the early 1920s: in 1922 Mr. Coates still led the field with his famous Rufflyn Danes, although Mr. Rank had that year made a favourable start. It was 1923 when Ouborough began to take the lead, and it was not until 1926 that Mr. Gordon Stewart won his first Challenge Certificate with Brenda of Send.

In 1927 fifteen C.C.s went to Ouborough, and in 1928 the Send Danes had the new Ch. Hermione of Send to their credit. The year 1929 saw Send with ten and Ouborough with eleven C.C.s; then in 1930 the lead was taken by Send, who won eighteen C.C.s to Ouborough's four.

Keen rivalry continued between these two giants—results in 1931 shows Ouborough with nine and Send with fourteen C.C.s. In 1932 Ouborough took the lead again with twelve C.C.s to Send's four, while 1933 saw Ouborough still maintaining its supremacy with fifteen C.C.s going to their dogs as compared with only three awarded to Send. Ouborough continued to hold the lead, and in 1934 managed to annex twenty more C.C.s as against Send's total of six. In 1935 the black Ch. Rahie of Send won a C.C., but in 1936 we find no mention of Send among the winners, although in 1937 a harlequin by the name of Ivor of Send did win a C.C.

Meanwhile Ouborough seemed to have established their supremacy beyond all doubt, for in 1935 their grand record was twenty-three C.C.s, 1936 brought a further eight, and in 1937 the total numbered sixteen.

I have devoted some considerable space to these two famous kennels, for in their heyday their like had not been seen before, and it is unlikely that we shall see their equal in the future. For some years they monopolised Great Dane breeding and showing, but at the same time there were smaller successful breeders who were also making their mark, and many of these took the opportunity to use the valuable stud dogs which had been imported. The small breeders are always the backbone of the fancy, and at that time there were a number who made quite a name for themselves. Mrs. Elliott (Miss Callinder) was breeding some very good dogs under her Bellary affix in the early 1920s. At the same time Mrs. Hatfield of the famous Sudbury harlequins, who established her kennel in 1906, was recognised as one of the best harlequin breeders of all time; she had a flair for breeding this, the most difficult of all colours of any breed, and succeeded where others who spent fortunes were not nearly so successful.

Mr. Whitney of the famous Primley Danes had been in the top flight since 1910, one of his best-known dogs being Ch. Primley Prodigal, and he was still holding his own at the shows in the 1920s. Mr. Coates of 'Rufflyn' fame and Mrs. Napier-Clavering of 'Axwell' were notable names associated with Great Danes. Then there were Miss Davy of 'Arnoldsfield' (who formerly showed her Danes under the name of 'Wellwyn'), Mr. Scuffman of 'Blundell', Mrs. Jones of 'Canis Major', Mrs. Knight of 'Cuckmere', Mrs. C. Robb of 'Foxbar', Miss Startin of 'Gammaton', Mrs. Sprosen of 'Oughton', the Hon. Mrs. Phillips of 'Phillipine', Mr. John Silver of 'Silvermia', Mrs. Lee Booker of 'Trayshill' and so on; they all contributed by consistently breeding good stock. It was in 1930 that Miss Muriel Osborn of 'Blendon' fame won her first C.C. with the beautiful bitch which was soon to become Ch. Bedina of Blendon, and was to be the forerunner of one of the most famous lines in the breed.

Miss Startin was another enthusiast who made quite an impression with her 'Gammatons'; Miss Davy's Arnoldsfield Amelia, Carola and Christopher all won C.C.s in 1935, and Miss Evans had a very good youngster in Regal of Windale, which unfortunately died at an early age from distemper.

Miss Mansell was well known for her harlequins, Mrs. R. M. Hill (formerly Mrs. Jones) produced a home-bred champion in Jason of Canis Major, while Major Telfer Dunbar—who had done well with his 'Lavrocks'—in 1937 made up a champion fawn bitch in Billie of Lavrock. Mrs. Connie Robb had a very good fawn in Ch. Rebel of Foxbar, and was another who was consistently breeding a good type of Great Dane.

Few kennels over the years have specialised solely in blues and blacks. In earlier times Mrs. Cowan established the famous

'Rungmook' fawns and blues, and later went to Canada where she was very successful. Names such as Clifford Slack, Mrs. Blackler, Mr. Hall, Mr. Houston and Miss Stevenson will always be associated with the black variety. To breed blacks and blues to the standard of excellence of the fawns and brindles has always been a challenge which few people have been prepared to take up.

It would seem that in the 1930s there were problems similar to those which we find today. Quoting from Mrs. Lee Booker's book, in stating her views on the Great Danes in the 1930s she says:

'Soundness is, above all, the thing to aim at and the point in which British Danes excel—that and movement. It is highly dangerous to mate unsound Danes. At the same time, only a handful of breeders know what soundness really is; they tend to call a dog which moves "well", sound, when they ignore the faulty croup, loaded or steep shoulders, the curved spine or the incorrect set-on of tail. The bad fault of "pinning-in", we have actually heard praised! The dog which toes-in, also elbows-out, and probably plaits with his front legs. But how we all admire the Dane which strides along, his joints appearing to move in well-oiled ball bearings, each limb extended to the utmost, and every muscle being called into use.'

Further comments from Mrs. Lee Booker also prove interesting. She had this to say on judges of the 1930s:

'All judges have their fancies, and peculiarities. The trouble is there are too many shows, and not enough expert judges. Every judge has to make a start sometime, and one must not expect perfection at once. Judges stand to make one friend per class and many enemies!

It might, however, be a good time to call all judges together once a year, to come to a general understanding of standard, under which they are being invited to judge.'

Many of these comments on dogs and judges in the 1930s could well apply today.

In Milo Denlinger's book *The Complete Great Dane* there are some interesting remarks on pre-war Danes in England. Reporting on the findings of a Swiss judge who officiated in England in 1938, he says:

'The Great Danes in England are conspicious because of their enormous size and splendid walk. I saw giants there which cannot be duplicated on the continent, but one-tenth of them had some faults in their jaws. In their walk 90 per cent were good, and the same was true of the shape of the forehand and hindquarters. Some cow-hocks were evident, and some heads were rather flat to the little stop. Tops of noses were too narrow, and head lines float backwards too much. The harlequins were first class as to colour.'

It seems that in 1938 British Great Danes presented a pleasing picture for make, shape and balance, but that improvement in head and mouth was called for, in many cases.

During the 1930s the breeders seem to have enjoyed being involved in controversy. Many of the Great Dane breed notes from the columns of *Our Dogs* of those times tell an interesting story. In 1931 correspondence became so lively as to what was 'the correct type' that Mrs. Violet Horsfall of the famous 'Redgraves', although inactive as a breeder and exhibitor for twenty-five years, was prompted to write. In a letter to the editor of *Our Dogs* headed 'Great Dane Type' she wrote:

'Sir,
As my Great Dane affix was "Redgrave" I write to say that the letter in your issue of January 2nd signed by this *nom de plume* was not written by me. I am not in a position to criticise Mr. Gordon Stewart's remarks, as I attend dog shows so seldom; but as regards his reference to pre-war dogs, perhaps his knowledge does not go back as far as mine! I began breeding Danes in 1892, and not finding the type I admired in England, I imported "Hannibal of Redgrave" and his mother, "Emma", from Holland; the latter was due in whelp to a beautiful dog "Bosco Colonia". Judging from photographs, I do not think

any Dane of today can equal those three (and some of their descendants) for beauty of outline, carriage and general appearance. The keen, eager, alert expression seems wanting in Danes nowadays. When I judged at the Crystal Palace a few years ago, I thought the Danes of a much heavier type than in my day. They were no taller, but so much more massive, and nearly all lacking that expression of keen eagerness. It must be remembered that cropping was abolished very soon after I started breeding Great Danes, yet I have several of my un-cropped dogs, showing that keen, eager expression. A Dane must be a big dog, but I think a lot in the way of grace, ability and beauty of outline has been sacrificed to mere size.

Yours etc.,

Violet Horsfall'

A letter coming at this time from such an eminent authority as Mrs. Horsfall must have carried a great deal of weight. Here was an expert who had no axe to grind, and had been acknow-ledged by other experts as having had some of the best Great Danes ever. She was also at an advantage in that she had seen so many of the early notable German Great Danes, and was there-fore commenting from first-hand experience. I feel this letter, which she wrote over forty years ago, could be read again and again by present-day students of the breed, for her comments still apply today.

During these years the three Breed Clubs, namely the Great Dane Club, the Northern Great Dane and the Great Dane Breeders' Association, all played important roles in furthering the interests of the breed. Specialist shows were regularly organised, and the Great Dane Breeders' Association—being the newer club —was extremely lively, and organised shows in various parts of the country nearly every month. Indeed, we can find frequent references, in the Breed Notes of the day, to parties travelling from London to Stafford for 16s. 9d. return, with an extra charge of 4s. 9d. for dogs!

In the 1930s there seemed to be more excitement in the breed than today. One highlight was in 1931, when Mr. and Mrs. Rank exhibited two dogs at the great Westminster Show held annually in New York, which is on a parallel with our Cruft's. A winner in this country, Faun of Ouborough (sire of Ch. Ruffler of Ouborough), and Rhena v.d. Rheinschange (sired by the world-famous Ch. Dolf v.d. Saalburg) both competed at this important international show. They were left in America, where they gained their American titles.

Just prior to the outbreak of the Second World War there were something like 120 kennel names registered with the Kennel Club by fanciers interested in breeding Great Danes. Now, thirty years later, only two of them are still active in the breed. The Ouborough kennels passed over to the manager, Mr. W. G. Siggers, when founder Mr. J. V. Rank died in 1951. During his thirty years in charge of the breeding, rearing and handling of these dogs Mr. Siggers had had more than thirty Great Dane champions pass through his hands.

Miss Muriel Osborn, who bred her first champion in 1930, had many 'Blendon' champions in the 1946 post-war era. It was these two strains which were primarily responsible for getting the Great Dane on its feet again after the Second World War, following a severe setback caused by six years of hostilities, when breeding stock had become virtually non-existent.

Although many of the old breeders remained, few felt they could pick up the threads where they had left off. Many years of achievement in building up good strains were lost almost over-night, and to start again from scratch was for many an insur-mountable task. One famous pre-war breeder said to me, 'By 1938 I had reached the point of no return with my Great Danes, and did not feel I could possibly begin again to build a strain.'

Now a look at Germany, where the years between the wars were to prove some of the best for the Great Dane. Purchase of German stock was world-wide, for there was no doubt that there were many excellent dogs in the country of the breed's adoption.

Although many more Great Danes were bred in Germany than in England, emphasis was always on quality rather than quantity, and the *Deutsche Doggen Club* felt this was an essential part of their policy. High standards were set by the German club and therefore only attracted those with high ideals for the breed.

The stud male must be twenty months or older, and the breeding bitch must not be younger than eighteen months. Where a bitch is bred from under twenty months of age, she may rear only four puppies from her litter, and bitches which are over twenty months of age may rear only six puppies at a time. Further, brood bitches may only have one litter in twelve months. Breeders who fail to observe these regulations cannot have their breeder papers endorsed by the *Deutsche Doggen Club*.

There are many who would not agree with the severe ruling of the German club. However, it must be said in their favour that because such stringent regulations were laid down only the best stock was retained and therefore the breed prospered. It would seem that the main 'trunk of the tree' grew stronger and stronger because of the constant ruthless culling and pruning. Moreover, the *Deutsche Doggen Club* has always exercised responsibility and control, and periodical directives to both breeders and judges have always been in the best interests of the breed.

In England we would find such controlled breeding most difficult to accept, but I think this is one reason why Germany has always been successful in evolving breeds to a high standard. Many dogs and bitches which are regularly bred from in our country would, in fact, never be accepted for breeding purposes in Germany.

Germany was already breeding some very fine Great Danes, but a breakthrough came in the early 1920s when the fabulous 'Saalburg' Great Danes appeared. As one expert of that time said, 'They were the greatest thing that ever happened in Great Danes.' The owner was Karl Farber, who had a lovely bitch called Fauna Monguntia which was sired by the famous but intensely inbred German Ch. Famulus Hansa (which is in most English pedigrees). When mated to Ch. Bosco v.d. Saalburg, Fauna Monguntia produced Ch. Dolf v.d. Saalburg.

The 'Saalburgs' were what one looked for in one's ideal Great Dane, and Ch. Dolf v.d. Saalburg became a great stud dog, with champion offspring the world over; he was described at one time as 'the greatest champion sire in the world', and this line has had a most profound influence on Great Danes.

Dolf was a tall, proud, graceful animal, with no semblance of the coarseness of his ancestors, but great depth of brisket and a strong back. One of his most famous daughters, Ch. Ferguni v. Loheland, was bred back to her own sire and thus intensified the excellent type. This was the famous 'N' litter, and Ch. Nepa v. Loheland has in her turn greatly influenced the Great Dane of today.

Ch. Dolf also produced the world champion Kalandus v. Drachenstein, and his own sire was another great dog called Ch. Bosco v.d. Saalburg. Most of the fawns and brindles of this period were line-bred back to this strain, and they became the most important dogs on which the Germans continued to build their Great Danes prior to the Second World War.

Other famous lines were the 'Hexengolds', who had some particularly fine brindles, the 'Birkenhofs' and the 'v. Lohelands', all bred from the illustrious Saalburg line. These names are still to be found behind the best Great Danes in any part of the world today.

It must always be remembered that there are limitations to close breeding, although many strains have become famous in this way. There is a danger that whilst type may remain good, stamina may be lost, and this can only be recovered by suitable out-crossing. As I shall mention in the chapter on breeding, line-breeding, in-breeding and out-crossing are best left to the experts.

The years between the wars also saw great advances in America. Like England, they were buying readily from Germany, and many good imports went to the States and gained their title. In the early 1930s Harkness Edwards of the 'Walnut' kennels campaigned six imports to their American title. The two most famous were Ch. Fionne v. Loheland of Walnut Hall, and her litter sister Ch. Ferguni v. Loheland.

At about the same time Mr. R. P. Stevens of the famous 'Brae Tarn' kennels finished eight champions, six of these being imports. He owned three exceptionally good imported dogs in Ch. Nero Hexengold, his son Ch. Randolph Hexengold, and the great sire Ch. Czardus v. Eppelin Sprung-Norris, which will go down in Great Dane history as the sire of ten champions. Of the latter's ten champion children, the two most remarkable were Ch. Heide of Brae Tarn and Ch. Jansen of Brae Tarn, also bred by Mr. R. P. Stevens, and these animals carrying the best of the imported German blood-lines have formed the framework of the present American Great Danes.

Still the 'v. Lohelands' continued to come into America. Mr. H. M. Warren, Jnr., of the 'Warrendale' kennels, imported from Germany, and successfully campaigned to their American titles Ch. Nanda v. Loheland and Ch. James v. Loheland.

Another exceptionally good dog was Ch. Zorn v. Birkenhof, a large brindle dog which stood 36½ in. at the shoulders. Owned by Mr. and Mrs. Owen A. West, he had previously had the high honour of winning Best in Show at the German Sieger Show in 1936. Other great dogs of the 1930s were Ch. Kuno v. Freigericht, Ch. Steinbachers King and the outstanding Ch. King v. Lionheart. Bred in America, Ch. King had one of the most distinguished of all show careers. Born on 4th December 1936, he was the son of Ch. Odin v. Birkenhof out of Lady Hexengold. Bred by Mrs. W. D. Crews, he was described as being 'a medium-large, fawn, and a beautifully balanced dog'. His show career included thirteen times Best in Show, thirty-six Working Groups and seventy-one times Best of Breed. King was owned by Mr. and Mrs. William C. Field, of Cincinnati, Ohio.

Ch. Hansi of Garricrest was another eminent dog of this decade, owned and bred by Vincent J. Garrity. Hansi was also a fawn, medium-sized, with much elegance. Although shown only twenty-five times, he won eighteen Working Groups, fifteen Best in Shows, and was twenty-five times Best of Breed, therefore remaining unbeaten in his breed. At his last nine shows he remained completely undefeated by all comers from other breeds, and won Best of Breed at all these events.

At this time the breed was attracting more and more enthusiasts in the United States, as more people came to know and appreciate the qualities which had endeared the Great Dane to mankind for centuries.

Germany found a rich market in America, and many high-class dogs were exported and won the championships in the ring in the United States. One of the great happenings in American Great Dane history was when the beautiful German Ch. Etfa v. Saalburg was brought into the United States by Joseph Eigenbauer. Born on the 17 May 1925, and bred by Karl Farber, she was a fawn daughter of Ch. Bosco v.d. Saalburg and Fauna Moguntia, and was the same breeding which produced the immortal Ch. Dolf. Etfa was described as 'a truly great bitch', and even today there are many who rate her as one of the finest specimens ever seen. Etfa had already had a successful show career in Germany, having gained her German title, and this was to be followed by brilliant show-ring successes in the United States, the most important being Best of Breed at the Westminster Show held at Madison Square Garden, New York, in 1929. She proved also to be a great producing bitch, the mother of eight champions. To give you some idea of the influence that this particular bitch had on the breed in America, the winner of Best of Breed at the 1969 Westminster Show—Ch. Honey Gold von Overcup—has nineteen lines in her pedigree running directly back to Ch. Etfa v.d. Saalburg.

Ch. Eric Commodore is also worthy of a special mention; born on the 11th November 1922, he was bred by Mr. Steinbacher and later sold to Mr. and Mrs. Anderson of Cleveland, Ohio. Mr. Steinbacher, who had an extremely good line, considered Eric Commodore to be the best male he had ever bred, saying 'his head, there never has been one like it. He was big, and strong. There never was a dog to stand up to him. And with it all he had a real Dane disposition.' Ch. Eric Commodore was sired by Ch. Erick Pfaff and Ch. Thyla v.d. Rheinschanze. Others belonging to this famous breeder were Countess of Richmond, Burkes Count, Steinbachers Bertha, Steinbachers Midnight, Eric Chancellor, Rio Rita of Erindale and the dominant sire Peer Gynt. All were champions, and Peer Gynt had a considerable influence on the breed.

Other famous dogs in this decade between the 1920s and the 1930s were Ch. Ador Tipp Topp, a harlequin which won Westminster in 1924, also Ch. Argus v. Birkenhof.

Mr. Leith was a prominent breeder after the First World War, and in 1920 his dogs accounted for three of the four top wins. His best known dogs were Ch. Rolling Hill Eric II, Ch. Rolling Hill Iduna and Ch. Rolling Hill Vidor. A sensational show winner of the 1930s was Ch. Monarch of Halecroft, bred by Mr. D. H.

Hale, who also had the very good Ch. Major Yeast Foam Rehbach.

Having been initially successful in establishing the Great Dane as a 'beautiful animal', the German breeders between the wars succeeded in producing magnificent dogs which the world went to Germany to buy. There is no doubt that the blending of their leading strains has made a lasting mark on the breed wherever it may be found in the world today.

4

The Great Dane Standards

In many ways this is the most important chapter in the book, for the standard is the 'be-all and end-all' so far as the Great Dane is concerned. Without it we have nothing, for it is both our bible and our textbook. However long one may be associated with the breed, it is most important that continual reference should be made to the standard, for this is the blueprint of the Great Dane.

All breed standards in Great Britain are officially issued by the Kennel Club, the breed clubs having initially drafted out what they considered to be the ideal requirements. Seldom are amendments made, for the early pioneer breeders were people with high ideals who knew exactly what they wanted.

Based originally on the German standard, the American and British standards vary very little. The words and definitions used are not always identical, but the basic picture which emerges is common to all three, which I feel is a very happy state of affairs!

Great Dane fanciers, whether they be judges, breeders, or both, should always be fully conversant with the standard. It can never be read too often, and all judges—however much they think they know—should refer to their standard before a judging assignment.

I am reproducing all three standards, for the German has been our prototype and the American—in my opinion—is the most explicit and detailed. One cannot fail to understand conformation after studying the American standard, with its excellent illustrations which have been produced by the Great Dane Club of America.

Dogs must always be judged as a whole, and the immediate picture should be pleasing to the eye. Assuming that the animal is true to type, I feel that one's ideal Great Dane should give as much pleasure to the onlooker as a beautiful piece of music or a delightful painting. Just as a wrong note can bring discord which ruins the music, and one careless stroke of the brush can completely spoil the picture, so the ugly structural faults so common in present-day Danes can mar the whole appearance of the animal and detract from our appreciation.

We must therefore have balance, construction and soundness, for all three are relevant. Without these basic essentials, breeders are building their strains on sand, and while they may be producing animals which can win in their breed they will never succeed in breeding truly 'great' dogs, that is Great Danes capable of holding their own in the hottest competition with other breeds. It is indeed a sad state of affairs that in post-war England fewer than six Danes have been able to win Groups or Best in Show at our All-Breed Champion Events—not a very fine record in twenty-five years of breeding! During this time the breed has been more numerically strong than at any other time in its history, but perhaps the key to its present weakness lies in its popularity? There is no doubt that in many cases mass production of puppies has been the order of the day, with little attention given to selection.

I well remember one of our best-known judges running the rule over the breeds a few years ago. She commented that so many of the Great Danes looked as though a puff of wind would blow them over, and added that 'a Great Dane should be like a beautiful building, pleasant to look at but capable of standing up to the job'. This put the situation rather neatly in a nutshell.

My final advice to all Dane enthusiasts is to make a point of studying the best in other breeds. Do not be anxious to rush out of a show on your 'early removal' card; stay to see the Best in Show, and ask yourself, 'What is it about that dog which makes him a great animal?' Whether it be Chihuahua, Cocker Spaniel or Irish Wolfhound, they all have in common the same fundamental merits which have taken them to the top show award.

I now give the German, American and English standards in full, followed by my own personal comments on all three.

THE GERMAN GREAT DANE STANDARD

General Appearance and Character. The Great Dane combines pride, strength and elegance in its noble appearance and big, strong, well-coupled body. It is the Apollo of all the breeds of dogs. The Dane strikes one by its very expressive head; it does not show any nervousness even in the greatest excitement, and has the appearance of a noble statue. In temperament it is friendly, loving and affectionate with its masters, especially with children, but retiring and mistrustful with strangers. In time of danger the dog is courageous and not afraid of attacks, caring only for the defence of its master and the latter's property.

Head. Elongated, narrow, striking, full of expression, finely chiselled (especially the part under the eyes), with strongly accentuated stop. Seen from the side, the brow should be sharply broken off from the bridge of the nose. The forehead and bridge of the nose must run into each other in a straight and parallel line. Seen from the front, the head must appear narrow, the bridge of the nose must be as broad as possible; the cheek muscles should be only slightly accentuated, but in no case must they be prominent. The muzzle must be full of lip, as much as possible vertically blunted in front, and show well-accentuated lip-angle. The underjaw should be neither protruding nor retrograding. The forehead, from the tip of the nose to the stop, must as far as possible be of the same length as the back of the head, from the stop to the slightly accentuated occiput. Seen from all sides, the head should appear angular and settled in its outer lines, but at the same time it should harmonise entirely with the general appearance of the Great Dane in every way. *Faults*: Falling-off line of brow, an elevated, falling-off or compressed bridge of nose; too little or no stop; too narrow a bridge of nose; the back of the head wedge-shaped; too round a skull (apple head); cheeks too pronounced; snipy muzzle. Also loose lips hanging over the underjaw, which can be deceptive as to a full, deep muzzle. It is preferable for the head to be short and striking, rather than long, shallow and expressionless.

Eyes (in general). Of medium size, round, as dark as possible, with gay, hearty expression, the eyebrows well developed. *Faults:* Eyes light, cutting, amber-yellow, light blue or water blue, or of two different colours; too low-hanging eyelids with prominent tear glands or very red conjunctiva tunica.

Ears. Set on high, not too far apart, of good length, cropped to a point. *Faults:* Ears set on too low, laterally; cropped too short or not uniformly; standing too much over or even lying on the head; not carried erect or semi-drooping ears. (Uncropped Danes should not win.)*

Nose. Large, black, running in a straight line with the bridge. *Faults:* Nose light coloured, with spots, or cleft.

Teeth. Large and strong, white, fitting in to each other, which is correct when the lower incisors fit tightly into the upper ones just as two scissor blades. *Faults:* The incisors of the lower jaw are protruding (undershot) or those of the upper jaw protrude (overshot). Also, when the incisors of both jaws stand one upon another ('crackers'), for in this case the teeth wear out prematurely. Imperceptible deviations are allowed. Distemper teeth should be objected to as they hide caries; likewise when the teeth look broken or are brown. Tartar is also undesirable.

Neck. Long, dry, muscular and sinewy, without strongly developed skin or dewlap; it should taper slightly from the chest to the head, be nicely ascending, and set-on high with a well-formed nape. *Faults:* Neck short, thick with loose skin or dewlap.

Shoulders: The shoulder-blade should be long and slanting; it should join the bone of the upper arm in the same position in the shoulder joint, as far as possible forming a right angle, in order to allow roomy movement. The withers should be well accentuated. *Faults:* Straight or loose shoulders; the former occur when the shoulder-blade is not sufficiently slanting, the latter when the elbows turn outwards.

Chest. As large as possible, the ribs well rounded, deep in front, reaching up to the elbow joints. *Faults:* Chest narrow, shallow with flat ribs; chest bone protruding too much.

Body. The back straight, short and tight, the body should be

* Translator's note: Of course the above refers to cropped ears; with us the ears should be small.

Grand Ch. Rex Lendor von Zeltnerschloss of Ouborough

Ch. Record of Ouborough

Walter Guiver

Group of the famous Send Great Danes

Sally Anne Thompson

Jean Lanning with a group of Clausentums

Ch. Sarzec Blue Baron

Diane Pearce

Ch. Kaptain of Kilcroney

Hartley

Ch. Daneton Amilia

Jansken

Am. Ch. Senta

as far as possible square in relation to the height; a somewhat longer back is allowed in bitches. The loins should be lightly arched and strong, the crupper running fully imperceptibly into the root of the tail. The belly should be well tucked up backwards, and forming a nicely arched line with the inside of the chest. *Faults:* Saddle-back, roach-back, or when the height of the hindquarters exceeds that of the forequarters (overbuilt); too long a back, since the gait then suffers (rolling gait); the crupper falling off at a slant; belly hanging down and badly showing teats in bitches.

Tail. Of medium length, only reaching to the hocks, set on high and broad, but tapering to a point; hanging down straight at rest, slightly curved (sword-like) in excitement or in running, not carried over the back. *Faults:* Tail too long, too low set on, carried too high over the back, or curled over the back; turned sideways; broken off or docked (it is forbidden to shorten the tail to obtain the prescribed length); brush tail (when the hair on the inside is too long) is undesirable. It is forbidden to shave the tail.

Front Legs. The continuation of the elbows of the forearm must not reach the round of the chest, but must be well let down, must not appear either inwards or outwards, but should lie in equal flatness with the shoulder joint. The upper arms should be strong, broad and muscular, the legs strong and—seen from the front or the side—absolutely straight down to the pasterns. *Faults:* Elbows turning in or out; if turning in, their position impedes movement by rubbing against the ribs, and at the same time turns the whole lower part of the legs and causes the feet to turn outwards; if turning out, the reverse happens and the toes are forced inwards. Both these positions are at fault, but the latter does not hinder movement since it does not cause any rubbing of the elbows against the chest wall. If the forelegs stand too wide apart the feet are forced to turn inwards, while in the case of the 'narrow' stand brought about by the narrow chest, the front legs incline towards each other and the toes again turn outwards. The curving of the joint of the root of the front foot is equally faulty; it points to weakness in the pasterns (soft pasterns) or in foot-roots (tarsus), and often causes flat feet and splayed toes. Swelling over the joint of the tarsus points mainly to diseases of the bone (rickets).

Hind Legs. The buttocks of the hind legs should be broad and muscular, the under-thighs long, strong, and forming a not too obtuse angle with the short tarsus. Seen from behind, the hocks should appear absolutely straight, sloping neither outwards nor inwards. *Faults:* If the knee-joint is turned too far outwards, the under-thigh forces the hock inwards and the dog is then 'cow-hocked', not a nice position at all. Too broad a stand in the hocks is just as ugly, as it impedes the light movement. In profile, the well-developed hind thigh shows good angulation. A straight hind thigh is faulty, for there the under-thigh is too short and the dog is forced to keep it vertically to the straight tarsus. If the bone of the hind thighs is too long (in relation to the fore-limbs), then the hind thighs are diagonally bent together, and this is not at all good.

Feet. Roundish, turned neither inwards nor outwards. The toes should be short, highly arched and well closed, the nails short, strong and black. *Faults:* Splayed toes, hare-feet, toes turned inwards or outwards; further, the fifth toes on the hind legs placed higher (dew claw); also if the nails are too long, or light in colour.

Movement. Fleeting, stepping out. *Faults:* Short strides which are not free; narrow or rolling gait; ambling gait.

Coat. Very short and thick, lying close and shiny. *Faults:* Hair too long; lopped hair (due to bad feeding, worms and faulty care).

Colour

(a) *Brindle Danes:* Ground colour from light golden fawn to dark golden fawn, always with well-defined black stripes. The more intense the ground colour and the stronger the stripes, the more striking is the effect. Small white patches on the chest and toes, or light eyes and nails, are not desirable. *Faults:* Silver-blue or biscuit-coloured ground colour, washed-out stripes, white streak between the eyes up to the nose, white ring on the neck, white 'socks' and white tip of tail. Danes with such white markings should be excluded from winning prizes.

(b) *Fawn Danes:* Colour, fawn-golden and fawn to dark golden fawn; black mask as well as black nails are desired.* The golden-fawn colour should always be preferred. *Faults:* Silver-grey, blue-grey, biscuit-fawn and dirty-fawn colour should be placed lower in the award list. For white markings, see (a) above.

(c) *Blue Danes*: The colour should be as far as possible steel blue, without any tinge of fawn or black. Lighter eyes are allowed in blue Danes. *Faults:* Fawn-blue or black-blue colour, too light or wall eyes. Regarding white markings, see (a) above.

(d) *Black Danes:* Should be wallflower black, shiny, with dark eyes and black nails. *Faults:* Yellow-brown or blue-black colour; light or amber-coloured eyes; lightly coloured nails. Danes with too many white markings should be lower in the list of awards. Under white markings it should be noted that a white streak on the throat, spots on the chest, on toes (only up to the pasterns) are allowed, but Danes with a white blaze, white ring on the neck, white 'socks' or white belly, should be debarred from winning.

(e) *Harlequins:* The ground colour should always be white, without any spots, with patches running all over the body, well-torn, irregular, wallflower black (a few small grey or brownish patches are admitted but not desired). Nose and nails should be black, but a nose with black spots or a fleshy nose are allowed. Eyes should be dark; light or two-coloured eyes are permitted but not desired. *Faults:* White ground colour with several large, black patches; bluish-grey ground colour; water-light, red or bleary eyes.

The following Danes should be excluded from winning:

1. White Danes without any black markings; albinos, as well as deaf Danes.

2. 'Mantle' harlequins, i.e. Danes having a large patch—like a mantle—running all over the body, and only the legs, neck and tip of the tail are white.

3. So-called 'porcelain' harlequins, i.e. Danes with mostly blue-grey, fawn or even brindle patches.

Size. The height at the shoulder should not be under 76 cm

* Translator's note: It will be seen that whereas a black mask in fawn Great Danes was formerly not desired, as reminding one of Mastiffs, it is now desired.

(1 in. is about 2½ cm), but preferably should measure about 80 cm; in bitches, not under 70 cm but preferably 75 cm and over.

THE AMERICAN GREAT DANE STANDARD

General Conformation

(a) *General Appearance.* The Great Dane combines in its distinguished appearance dignity, strength and elegance with great size and a powerful, well-formed, smoothly muscled body. He is one of the giant breeds, but it is unique in that his general conformation must be so well balanced that he never appears clumsy and is always a unit—the Apollo of dogs. He must be spirited and courageous—never timid. He is friendly and dependable. This physical and mental combination is the characteristic which gives the Great Dane the majesty possessed by no other breed. It is particularly true of this breed that there is an impression of great masculinity in dogs as compared with an impression of femininity in bitches. The male should appear more massive throughout than the bitch, with large frame and heavier bone. In the ratio between length and height, the Great Dane should appear as square as possible. In bitches a somewhat longer body is permissible. *Faults:* Lack of unity; timidity; bitchy dogs; poor musculature; poor bone development; out of condition; rickets; doggy bitches.

(b) *Colour and Markings*

(i) *Brindle Danes.* Base colour ranging from light golden yellow to deep golden yellow always brindled with strong black cross stripes. The more intensive the base colour and the more intensive the brindling, the more attractive will be the colour. Small white marks at the chest and toes are not desirable. *Faults:* Brindle with too dark a base colour; silver-blue and greyish-blue base colour; dull (faded) brindling; white tail tip.

(ii) *Fawn Danes.* Golden yellow up to deep golden yellow colour with a deep black mask. The golden deep-yellow colour must always be given the preference. Small white spots at the chest and toes are not desirable. *Faults:* Yellowish-grey, bluish-yellow, greyish-blue, dirty yellow colour (drab colour); lack of black mask.

(iii) *Blue Danes*. The colour must be a pure steel blue as far as possible without any tinge of yellow, black or mouse grey. *Faults:* Any deviation from a pure steel-blue colouration.

(iv) *Black Danes*. Glossy black. *Faults:* Yellow-black, brown-black or blue-black. White markings, such as stripes on the chest, speckled chest and markings on the paws, are permitted but not desirable.

(v) *Harlequin Danes*. Base colour: pure white with black torn patches irregularly and well distributed over the entire body; pure white neck preferred. The black patches should never be large enough to give the appearance of a blanket nor so small as to give a stippled or dappled effect. (Eligible but less desirable are a few small grey spots, also pointings where instead of a pure white base with black spots there is a white base with single black hairs showing through which tend to give a salt and pepper or dirty effect.) *Faults:* White base colour with a few large spots; bluish-grey pointed background.

(c) *Size*. The male should not be less than 30 in. at the shoulders, but it is preferable that he be 32 in. or more, provided he is well proportioned to his height. The female should not be less than 28 in. at the shoulders, but it is preferable that she be 30 in. or more, provided she is well proportioned to her height.

(d) *Condition of Coat*. The coat should be very short and thick, smooth and glossy. *Faults:* Excessively long hair (stand-off coat); dull hair (indicating malnutrition, worms and negligent care).

(e) *Substance*. Substance is that sufficiency of bone and muscle which rounds out a balance with the frame. *Faults:* Lightweight whippety Danes; coarse, ungainly proportioned Danes; always there should be balance.

Movement

(a) *Gait*. Long, easy, springy stride with no tossing or rolling of body. The back line should move smoothly, parallel to the ground. The gait of the Great Dane should denote strength and power. The rear legs should have drive. The forelegs should track smoothly and straight. The Dane should track in two parallel straight lines. *Faults:* Short steps. The rear quarters should not pitch. The forelegs should not have a hackney gait (forced or choppy stride). When moving rapidly the Great Dane should not pace for the reason that it causes excessive side-to-side rolling of the body and thus reduces endurance.

(b) *Rear End* (*Croup, Legs, Paws*). The croup must be full, slightly drooping and must continue imperceptibly to the tail root. Hind legs, the first thighs (from hip joint to knee) are broad and muscular. The second thighs (from knee to hock joint) are strong and long. Seen from the side, the angulation of the first thigh with the body, of the second thigh with the first thigh, and the pastern root with the second thigh should be very moderate, neither too straight nor too exaggerated. Seen from the rear, the hock joints appear to be perfectly straight, turned neither towards the inside nor towards the outside. *Faults:* A croup which is too straight; a croup which slopes downward too steeply; and too narrow a croup. Hind legs: Soft, flabby, poorly muscled thighs; cowhocks which are the result of the hock joint turning inward and the hock and rear paws turning outward; barrel legs, the result of the hock joints being too far apart; steep rear. As seen from the side, a steep rear is the result of the angles of the rear legs forming almost a straight line; overangulation is the result of exaggerated angles between the first and second thighs and the hocks, and is very conducive to weakness. The rear legs should never be too long in proportion to the front legs.

Paws should be round and turned neither towards the inside nor towards the outside. Toes short, highly arched and well closed. Nails short, strong and as dark as possible. *Faults:* Spreading toes (splay foot); bent, long toes (rabbit paws); toes turned towards the outside or towards the inside. Furthermore, the fifth toe on the hind legs appearing at a higher position and with wolf's claw or spur; excessively long nails; light-coloured nails.

(c) *Front End* (*Shoulders, Legs, Paws*)

Shoulders: The shoulder-blades must be strong and sloping and seen from the side, must form as nearly as possible a right angle in its articulation with the humerus (upper arm) to give a long stride. A line from the upper tip of the shoulder to the back of the elbow joint should be as nearly perpendicular as possible. Since all dogs lack a clavicle (collar-bone), the ligaments and muscles holding the shoulder-blade to the rib-cage must be well developed, firm and secure to prevent loose shoulders. *Faults:* Steep shoulders, which occur if the shoulder-blade does not slope sufficiently; overangulation; loose shoulders which occur if the Dane is flabby muscled, or if the elbow is turned towards the outside; loaded shoulders.

Forelegs: The upper arm should be strong and muscular. Seen from the side or front the strong arms run absolutely straight to the pastern points. Seen from the front, the forelegs and the pastern roots should form perpendicular lines to the ground. Seen from the side, the pastern root should slope only very slightly forward. *Faults:* Elbows turned towards the inside or towards the outside, the former position caused mostly by too narrow or too shallow a chest, bringing the front legs too closely together and at the same time turning the entire lower part of the leg outward; the latter position causes the front legs to spread too far apart, with the pastern roots and paws usually turned inwards. Seen from the side, a considerable bend in the pastern towards the front indicates weakness and is in most cases connected with stretched and spread toes (splay foot); seen from the side a forward bow in the forearm (chair leg); an excessive bulge on the front of the pastern joint.

Paws: Round and turned neither towards the inside nor towards the outside. Toes short, highly arched and well closed. Nails short, strong and as dark as possible. *Faults:* Spreading toes (splay foot), bent, long toes (rabbit paws); toes turned towards the outside or towards the inside; light-coloured nails.

Head

(a) *Head Conformation.* Long, narrow, distinguished, expressive, finely chiselled, especially the part below the eyes (which means that the skull plane under and to the inner point of the eye must slope without any bony protuberance in a pleasing line to the full square jaw), with strongly pronounced stop. The masculinity of the male is very pronounced in the expression and structure of head (this subtle difference should be evident in the dog's head through massive skull and depth of muzzle); the bitch's head may be more delicately formed. Seen from the side, the forehead must be sharply set off from the bridge of the nose. The forehead and the bridge of the nose must be straight and parallel to one another. Seen from the front, the head should appear narrow, the bridge of the nose should be as broad as possible. The cheek muscles must show slightly but under no circumstances should they be too pronounced (cheeky). The muzzle part must have full flews and must be as blunt vertically as possible in front; the angles of the lip must be quite pronounced. The front part of the head, from the tip of the nose up to the centre of the stop, should be as long as the rear part of the head from the centre of the stop to the only slightly developed occiput. The head should be angular from all sides and should have definite flat planes and its dimensions should be absolutely in proportion to the general appearance of the Dane. *Faults:* Any deviation from the parallel planes of skull and foreface; too small a stop; a poorly defined stop or none at all; too narrow a nose bridge; the rear of the head spreading laterally in a wedgelike manner (wedge head); an excessively round upper head (apple head); excessively pronounced cheek musculature; pointed muzzle; loose lips hanging over the lower jaw (fluttering lips) which create an illusion of a full deep muzzle. The head should be rather shorter and distinguished than long and expressionless.

(b) *Teeth.* Strong, well developed and clean. The incisors of the lower jaw must touch very lightly the bottoms of the inner surface of the upper incisors (scissors bite). If the front teeth of both jaws bite on top of each other, they wear down too rapidly. *Faults:* Even bite; undershot and overshot; incisors out of line; black or brown teeth; missing teeth.

(c) *Eyes.* Medium size, as dark as possible, with lively intelligent expression; almond-shaped eyelids, well-developed eyebrows. *Faults:* Light-coloured, piercing, amber-coloured, light blue to a watery blue, red or bleary eyes; eyes of different colours; eyes too far apart; Mongolian eyes; eyes with pronounced haws; eyes with excessively drooping lower eyelids. In blue and black Danes, lighter eyes are permitted but are not desirable. In harlequins the eyes should be dark. Light-coloured eyes, two eyes of different colour and wall-eyes are permitted but not desirable.

(d) *Nose*. The nose must be large and in the case of brindled and single-coloured Danes, it must always be black. In harlequins the nose should be black; a black spotted nose is permitted; a pink-coloured nose is not desirable.

(e) *Ears*. Ears should be high, set not too far apart, medium in size, of moderate thickness, drooping forward close to the cheek. Top line of folded ear should be about level with the skull. *Faults:* hanging on the side, as on a Foxhound; cropped ears; high set, not set too far apart, well pointed but always in proportion to the shape of the head and carried uniformly erect.

Torso

(a) *Neck*. The neck should be firm and clean, high-set, well arched, long, muscular and sinewy. From the chest to the head, it should be slightly tapering, beautifully formed, with well-developed nape. *Faults:* Short, heavy neck, pendulous throat folds (dewlaps).

(b) *Loin and Back*. The withers form the highest part of the back, which slopes downward slightly towards the loins which are imperceptibly arched and strong. The back should be short and tensely set. The belly should be well shaped and tightly muscled, and, with the rear part of the thorax, should swing in a pleasing curve (tuck-up). *Faults:* Receding back; sway back; camel or roach back; a back line which is too high at the rear; an excessively long back; poor tuck-up.

(c) *Chest*. Chest deals with that part of the thorax (rib-cage) in front of the shoulders and front legs. The chest should be quite broad, deep and well muscled. *Faults:* A narrow and poorly muscled chest; strong protruding sternum (pigeon breast).

(d) *Ribs and Brisket*. Deals with that part of the thorax back of the shoulders and front legs. Should be broad, with the ribs sprung well out from the spine and flattened at the side to allow proper movement of the shoulders extending down to the elbow joint. *Faults:* narrow (slab-sided) rib-cage; round (barrel) rib-cage; shallow rib-cage not reaching the elbow joint.

(e) *Tail*. Should start high and fairly broad, terminating slender and thin at the hock joint. At rest, the tail should fall straight. When excited or running, slightly curved (saberlike). *Faults:* A too high or too low-set tail (the tail set is governed by the slope of the croup); too long or too short a tail; tail bent too far over the back (ring tail); a tail which is curled; a twisted tail (sideways); a tail carried too high over the back (gay tail); a brush tail (hair too long on lower side). Cropping tails to desired length is forbidden.

Faults

Disqualification Faults. Deaf Danes. Danes under minimum height. White Danes without any black marks (albinos). Merles, a solid mouse-grey colour or a mouse-grey base with black or white or both colour spots or white base with mouse-grey spots. Harlequins and solid-coloured Danes in which a large spot extends coatlike over the entire body so that only the legs, neck and the point of the tail are white. Brindle, fawn, blue and black Danes with white forehead line, white collar, high white stockings and white bellies. Danes with predominantly blue, grey, yellow or also brindled spots. Docked tails. Split noses.

The faults below are important according to their grouping (very serious, serious, minor) and not according to their sequence as placed in each grouping:

Very serious: Lack of unity. Poor bone development. Poor musculature. Lightweight whippety Danes. Rickets. Timidity. Bitchy dog. Sway-back. Roach back. Cow-hocks. Pitching gait. Short steps. Under-shot teeth.

Serious: Out of condition. Coarseness. Any deviation from the standard on all colouration. Deviation from parallel planes of skull and foreface. Wedge head. Poorly defined stop. Narrow nose bridge. Snipy muzzle. Any colour but dark eyes in fawns and brindles. Mongolian eyes. Missing teeth. Overshot teeth. Heavy neck. Short neck. Dewlaps. Narrow chest. Narrow rib-cage. Round rib-cage. Shallow rib-cage. Loose shoulders. Steep shoulders. Elbows turned inward. Chair legs (front). Knotty bulge in pastern joint (adult dog). Weak pastern roots. Receding back. Too long a back. Back high in rear. In harlequins, a pink nose. Poor tuck-up (except in bitches that have been bred). Too straight croup. Too sloping croup. Too narrow croup. Over-angulation. Steep rear. Too long rear legs. Poorly muscled thighs. Barrel legs. Paws turned outward. Rabbit paws. Wolf's claw. Hackney gait.

Minor: Doggy bitches. Small white marks on chest and toes—blues, blacks, brindles and fawns. Few grey spots and pointings on harlequins. In harlequins, black-spotted nose. White-tipped tail except on harlequins. Excessively long hair. Excessively dull hair. Apple head. Small stop. Fluttering lips. Eyes too far apart. Drooping lower eyelids. Haws. Any colour but dark eyes in blacks, blues and harlequins. Discoloured teeth. Even bite. Pigeon breast. Loaded shoulders. Elbows turned outward. Paws turned inward. Splay foot. Excessively long toenails. Light nails (except in harlequins). Low-set tail. Too long a tail. Too short a tail. Gay tail. Twisted tail. Brush tail.

Disqualifications

Danes under minimum height. White Danes without any black marks (albinos). Merles, a solid mouse-grey colour or a mouse-grey base with black or white or both colour spots or white base with mouse-grey spots. Harlequins and solid-coloured Danes in which a large spot extends coatlike over the entire body so that only the legs, neck and the point of the tail are white. Brindle, fawn, blue and black Danes with white forehead line, white collars, high white stockings and white bellies. Danes with predominantly blue, grey, yellow or also brindled spots. Docked tail. Split noses.

Approved 14th November 1944

THE KENNEL CLUB GREAT DANE STANDARD
(Reproduced by permission of the Kennel Club)

General Appearance. The Great Dane should be remarkable in size and very muscular, strongly though elegantly built; the head and neck should be carried high, and the tail in line with the back, or slightly upwards but not curled over the hindquarters. Elegance of outline and grace of form are most essential to a Dane; size is absolutely necessary, but there must be that alertness of expression and briskness of movement without which the Dane character is lost. He should have a look of dash and daring, of being ready to go anywhere and do anything. The action should be lithe, springy and free, the hocks move freely and the head be carried high except when galloping.

Head and Skull. The head, taken altogether, should give the idea of great length and strength of jaw. The muzzle or foreface is broad, and the skull proportionately narrow, so that the whole head, when viewed from above in front, has the appearance of equal breadth throughout. The entire length of head varies with the height of the dog; 13 in. from the tip of the nose to the back of the occiput is a good measurement for a dog of 32 in. at the shoulder. The length from the end of the nose to the point between the eyes should be about equal, or preferably of greater length than from this point to the back of the occiput. The skull should be flat and have a slight indentation running up the centre, the occipital peak not prominent. There should be a decided rise or brow over the eyes but not an abrupt stop between them; the face should be well chiselled, well filled in below the eyes with no appearance of being pinched; the foreface long, of equal depth throughout. The cheeks should show as little lumpiness as possible, compatible with strength. The underline of the head, viewed in profile, should run almost in a straight line from the corner of the lip to the corner of the jawbone, allowing for the fold of the lip, but with no loose skin to hang down. The bridge of the nose should be very wide, with a slight ridge where the cartilage joins the bone. (This is a characteristic of the breed.) The nostrils should be large, wide and open, giving a blunt look to the nose. A butterfly or flesh-coloured nose is not objected to in harlequins. The lips should hang squarely in front, forming a right angle with the upper-line of foreface.

Eyes. Fairly deep set, of medium size and preferably dark. Wall or odd eyes permissible in harlequins.

Ears. Should be small, set high on the skull and carried slightly erect with the tips falling forward.

Mouth. The teeth should be level and not project one way or the other.

Neck. The neck should be long, well arched, and quite clean and free from loose skin, held well up, well set in the shoulders, and the junction of the head and neck well defined.

Forequarters. The shoulders should be muscular but not loaded, and well sloped back, with the elbows well under the body. The forelegs should be perfectly straight with big bone, which must be flat.

Body. The body should be very deep, with ribs well sprung and belly well drawn up. The back and loins should be strong, the latter slightly arched.

Hindquarters. The hindquarters and thighs should be extremely muscular, giving the idea of great strength and galloping power. The second thigh is long and well developed, the stifle and hock well bent, the hocks set low, turning neither in nor out.

Feet. The feet should be catlike and should not turn in or out. The toes well arched and close, the nails strong and curved. Nails should be black, but light nails are permissible in harlequins.

Tail. The tail should be thick at the root and taper towards the end, reaching to or just below the hocks. It should be carried in a straight line level with the back, when the dog is in action, slightly curved towards the end, but in no case should it curl or be carried over the back.

Coat. The hair is short and dense and sleek-looking, and in no case should it be inclined to roughness.

Colour. (a) Brindles must be striped, ground colour from the lightest yellow to the deepest orange, and the stripes must always be black. Eyes and nails preferably dark.

(b) Fawns; the colour varies from lightest buff to deepest orange, darker shading on the muzzle and ears and around the eyes are by no means objectionable. Eyes and nails preferably dark.

(c) Blues; the colour varies from light grey to deepest slate.

(d) Blacks; black is black.

(In all the above colours white is only admissible on the chest and feet, but is not desirable even there. The nose is always black (except in blues). Eyes and nails preferably dark.)

(e) Harlequins; pure white underground, with preferably black patches (blue patches permitted), having the appearance of being torn. In harlequins, wall eyes, pink noses or butterfly noses are permissible but not desirable.

Weight and Size. The minimum height of an adult dog over eighteen months must be 30 in., that of a bitch 28 in. Weight: the minimum weight of an adult dog over eighteen months should be 120 lb, that of a bitch 100 lb.

Faults. Cow-hocks. Out at elbows. Straight stifles. Undershot or overshot mouth. Round bone. Snipy muzzle. Straight shoulders. Shell body. Ring tail.

Note. Male animals should have two apparently normal testicles fully descended into the scrotum.

I will take the points singly, my remarks being purely personal.

General Appearance. The Germans say that the Great Dane must be 'big', the Americans say 'great size', whilst the English say 'remarkable in size'. But when all these standards call for dogs of great size, what do they mean? Great compared with what? I feel that a Great Dane should always be a huge animal, but nowadays are we not getting size and height rather mixed?

All three standards require a minimum height to the shoulder of not less than 30 in. for a male, but a dog of this size would be laughed out if brought into the show-ring at the present time.

Nowadays people frequently claim that their dogs measure 38 and 39 in. at the shoulder. This may well be so, but what is the use of this height if the same animals are hopelessly straight in the shoulder? It is far better to have a dog of 34 or 35 in. (still a very good size) which has correctly laid shoulders. So a warning to newcomers: do not think that because your dog is big he is necessarily going to be the best! Alas, this is seldom the case.

It is important to remember here that we are now regularly breeding Great Danes which are 6–8 in. over the minimum standard. Yet I feel that at this point in the history of the Great Dane in England, we would do well to concentrate on improving the overall standard and not worry unduly about height, which we have in any case achieved. It is regrettable that the mad craze for breeding tall Danes has produced many narrow-fronted, flat-sided specimens, which are so untypical of the breed.

According to an article written in the early 1930s when the famous Send kennels were reviewed, the average height of a male Great Dane was then 30 in. In other words, the average height has increased by 4–5 in. in a mere forty years, and with this increase in height the size of the whole animal has correspondingly grown.

If breeders do not reach what they consider to be a desirable height and call a halt at this stage, it may mean that within the next three or four decades it would be possible to have dogs measuring upwards of 43 in. at the shoulder! As I see it, this would not be in the eventual interest of the breed, because the Dane will become so large that he can no longer fulfil his role as a companion. For the Great Dane today is already an extra-large dog by most standards.

The American standard completely clarifies the importance of balance, making shape, when it says 'that his general conformation must be so well balanced that he never appears clumsy, and is always a unit'. It is common to see dogs that are far from being a 'unit'; in fact one would describe them as unco-ordinated, giving the appearance of having been put together from ill-fitting parts.

Another important distinction clearly called for in the American

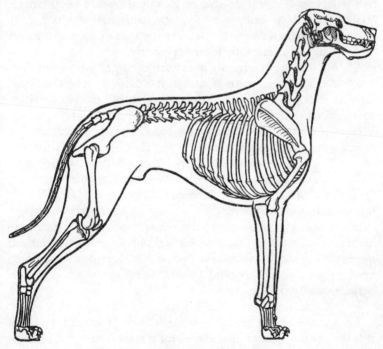

FIG. 1   Skeleton of a Great Dane

standard is that the male must be a more massive animal than the
bitch, with a larger frame and heavier bone. This is, in fact, what
one expects and looks for in most breeds of dog, but so often
the 'doggy' bitch is admired and wins high prizes. The dog should
always be strong and powerful, the bitch feminine and beautiful,
and both should combine the elegance and substance which is
called for in all three standards.

A famous all-rounder once said that a good dog should be able
to stand on a base of a triangle, one side of the triangle passing
through the correctly laid shoulders, the other side passing up
through the quarter. If the dog is correctly balanced and made,
the apex of the triangle will meet directly over the centre of the
top of the dog (see Fig. 1).

For myself, I like to see a dog standing four-square naturally,
and giving the impression that he is so beautifully constructed and
balanced, that if one were able to pick him up and drop him he
could not fail to land correctly, and with his whole weight
equally distributed on his four legs. (A glance at the photograph
of Ch. Senta illustrates my meaning exactly.)

All the standards give us a picture of dignity and nobility,
and both the American and German standards refer to the Great
Dane as the 'Apollo of all breeds', an imposing description which
speaks volumes.

Head and Skull. The three standards are most explicit on this
point, and all clearly emphasise that the nose should be wide and
blunt. The English standard defines this explicitly, stating that
'there should be a slight ridge where the cartilage joins the bone,
for this is a characteristic of the breed'. Much of the Great Dane's
beauty is found in the beautifully chiselled head, but dogs with
excellent heads and little else to recommend them should not figure
highly amongst the prizewinners at the shows. An eminent
international judge wisely said that 'a dog does not walk on its
head', which should remind us that there are other essentials
besides quality of head alone.

Eyes. General agreement all round.

Ears. In Germany and America show dogs are cropped, but
it is interesting to note that even here the ears are required to be
'high set', which rather dispels the theory held in this country

Fig. 2 Muscles

Fig. 3 Heads
(a) correct dog's head (b) correct bitch's head

that foreign Great Danes are 'not bred for ears'. This belief appears to be incorrect, for a highly placed ear must be aimed for if the final result of the cropping is to be entirely satisfactory. The German standard even stresses that it is a fault for ears to be set 'too low'.

Mouth. There is no doubt that the German and American standards are far more exacting and detailed than the English in defining the correct mouth. I feel it is a pity that we have allowed our standard regarding mouths to remain slightly ambiguous, leading those who choose to say 'mouths do not matter'. At one time, when faulty mouths were rarely seen, perhaps a good Dane whose one fault was a bad mouth could win. Now, however, we are reaping the benefit of those who have been casual in their breed plans, for bad mouths have increased alarmingly. It is possible at a show today to find that one-third of the Great Dane entries have faulty mouths. Judging all breeds of dogs regularly, as I do, I find there is no other breed at present which has this problem to such a degree.

Bad mouths can be 'bred out', but only if the effort is made to do so. For—make no mistake—they are to a large extent hereditary, and have an unpleasant way of skipping a generation or two, and then reappearing later on with a vengeance.

Also, one must accept that deliberately to breed to bad mouths is faulty breeding; for the dog with a bad mouth—however good in other respects—will always be limited in his show successes.

Having had the opportunity to judge the breed several times in the United States I know that a faulty mouth is rarely seen there, and I am convinced that this is mainly due to the fact that it has been written into the American standard that *an undershot jaw is a serious fault*.

At present we have two types of faulty mouths in England: firstly the typical undershot jaw—this is when the bottom jaw is in advance of the top jaw; secondly, when the bottom teeth are crowded out, and the appearance of being undershot is given. The latter, I find, usually occurs when a dog is not so good in the head, and has a small 'mean' jaw, which is not large enough for the teeth to come through properly spaced.

Neck. All the standards say 'long and strong'. Besides being

FIG. 4   Ears
(a) correct size and placement   (b) too large and set too low

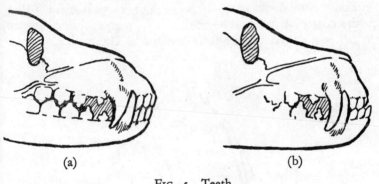

FIG. 5   Teeth
(a) correct scissor bite   (b) incorrect undershot

beautifully arched and as free from loose skin as possible, the junction of the neck and shoulders should blend beautifully; there should be no abruptness at this juncture.

Shoulders and Forequarters. The shoulders should be correctly laid back and when this happens the neck flows into them beautifully (see Figs. 1 and 2). No dog in any breed can be great without correct shoulders. One common fault is when the shoulder-blade is correctly laid but the humerus is too straight; another is when the humerus is correctly positioned but the shoulder-blade itself is upright. Dogs with this type of shoulder have often been said—quite wrongly—to be 'good in shoulder'. There must be a good slope of the humerus and the shoulder-blade which should meet at an angle of 90 degrees.

It is most important to have a correct shoulder, for this controls the whole balance of the animal. The dog which is straight in shoulder is inevitably shallow in brisket, the reason being that the entire rib-cage is carried too high. Where the shoulder is correctly placed, the rib-cage sits comfortably and the brisket comes to the elbow or thereabouts. Good shoulders are not the easiest part of the anatomy to recognise. If you stand directly in front of an animal, you should be able to see the chest and brisket quite clearly. A dog viewed from the front often has an empty space between the top of his front legs, when it is quite obvious there is no brisket; this is wrong, and would immediately point to faulty shoulder placing. It is common nowadays for a dog with a correct shoulder to be referred to as 'pigeon-chested', when in fact nothing is further from the truth. The problem at the

FIG. 6   Correct shoulder-blade placement and rib-cage

present time is that good shoulders are so rarely seen that in some quarters they are not readily appreciated.

Strangely enough, a straight shoulder and very upright head carriage go together, and so often provide the perfect pitfall for the novice judge! However, this is not to be confused with the proud head carriage and general bearing which typifies nobility.

The front legs, whether viewed from the front or side, should be absolutely straight. From the front they should be like two gun barrels, and present the appearance of running straight into the ground. From the side there should be the very slightest slope in the pastern—so slight as to be hardly noticeable, and not to be confused with a weak pastern. This very slight 'give' acts as a shock absorber when the dog is on the move, without which it is impossible to have the lithe springy action which is particularly defined in the British and American standards. The dog with the ultra-straight pastern will have either a hesitant or hackney gait, both of which are incorrect.

FIG. 7   Incorrect pigeon chest

Fig. 10 shows quite clearly a bowed or chair leg, a fault frequently encountered, but which so often escapes the eye of many judges.

Body and Chest. At the present time two of the worst faults to be seen in the English Great Dane are flat sides and narrow chests, so often accompanied by long backs which dip and sway. All three standards list these as faults, and the American standard also lists as a serious fault 'the round rib-cage'. This raises an interesting point, particularly for the newcomers to the breed. The ribs should be well sprung, gently graduating to a great depth of brisket (see Fig. 6). This is where the 'heart-room' is, and one has only to look at a good Greyhound to appreciate the correct rib-cage. Again, where a dog is too 'round in the rib-cage', he is consequently too wide in front and in the chest. Likewise, the 'flat rib-cage' goes with a narrow front.

Hindquarters. These should be extremely powerful, well muscled

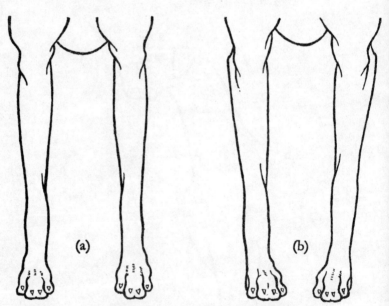

FIG. 8 Fronts (a) correct elbows, forelegs and feet
(b) incorrect elbows, turned out, feet turned in

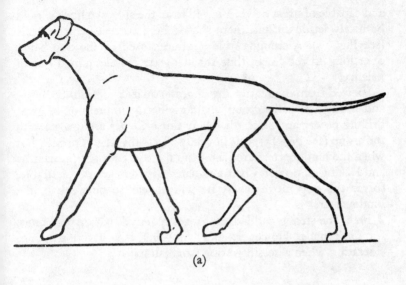

(a)

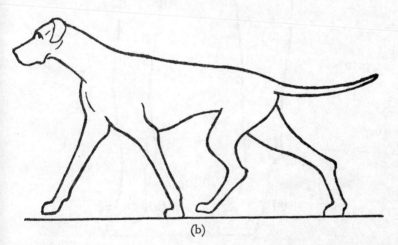

(b)

FIG. 9 Gait (a) correct trotting (b) incorrect pacing

and capable of great drive. Viewed from the side, the hock should be nicely let-down and there should be a correct bend of stifle (see Fig. 11). A straight stifle is often caused by the dog being over long in the hock, thus throwing the whole animal out of balance.

Viewed from the rear of the dog, the quarters should be broad and strong across the croup, again giving the impression of great driving power and strength. Many Great Danes are too steep in the croup (see Fig. 13); this not only affects the dog in profile, but when the hindquarters are seen from the rear they appear narrow and lacking in power. Over-angulated quarters are not desirable, for as the dog moves away he will appear to be weak in the hindquarters.

Feet. The strong padded cat-foot is required, with a preference for dark nails. However, nail colouring is a fractional consideration when assessing a dog's overall merit.

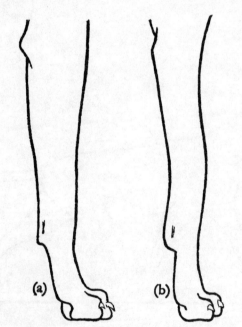

FIG. 10   Forelegs (a) correct   (b) incorrect, chair leg

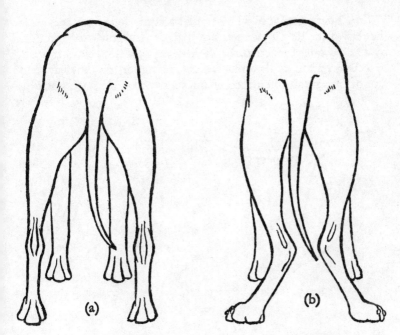

Fig. 11   Hindquarters: (a) correct   (b) cow hocks

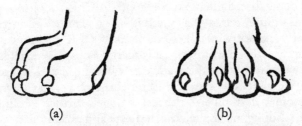

(a)   (b)

Fig. 12   Feet (a) well arched paw   (b) splay foot

Tail. There are those who say that a faulty tail is not serious if the rest of the dog is correct. But it all depends on what is meant by a faulty tail! I feel that the slightly gay tail—especially if it is a reflection of the dog's temperament—is rather nice anyway. But a poor, mean tail often accompanies a poor, mean dog. The dog

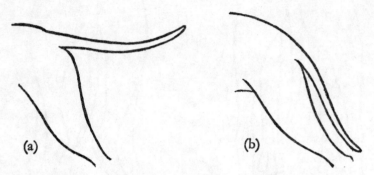

(a)   (b)

FIG. 13   Tails (a) correct set, alert   (b) too low set

with the correct quarters will also have a tail which is thick and strong at the root and correctly set on. The dog with narrow, weak quarters will usually have a thin 'whippety' tail, to complete them.

Coat. Short and shining. There is no substitute for good food and good grooming, and like all animals the coat of the dog is the 'barometer' of his health which is reflected by its condition.

Colour. Always seems to be open to controversy, although this is mainly due to personal preferences and dislikes. Firstly one must take the long view—that the Great Dane for type must always come first, and colour is secondary. This is not to say that colour is unimportant—for indeed it is not—and we all agree that mis-marks cannot win. Where some judges disagree, however, is on what exactly constitutes a 'mis-mark'. Some have stated that pale fawns are not in the standard, when in fact they are; the British Kennel Club standard quite clearly says that fawn may vary 'from palest buff to deepest orange', further adding that 'darker shadings on the muzzle and ears and around the eyes are by no means objectionable'. Yet there are those who will tell us that black masks are a 'must' in this country! There is nothing whatsoever in our standard to suggest this.

The Americans do call for a black mask as being desirable, but again they have been extremely wise in making a special point in the list of faults, clearly stating (except in harlequins) that only Danes with white forehead lines (a blaze), white bellies and white stockings should be disqualified. This gives a leader to a judge when sorting out his dogs.

A judge who may give a second prize to a dog, because he does not like his colour, is not a good judge. The animal should either be accepted as correct to the standard, and win accordingly, or else be recorded as a mis-mark and asked to retire from the ring. One cannot 'sit on the fence' on these issues.

It is interesting to note that right down the years of show Great Danes, some of the best of the breed in Germany, America and England have at one time or other been criticised for their colour. How fortunate that sane influences prevail, and that these lovely animals were fully appreciated and played their vital role of improving the breed.

(a) *Harlequins*. The harlequin is the most difficult colour to produce in any breed. But this has been so throughout the years, and I feel that those who choose to breed harlequins do so because they like the challenge this difficult colour presents.

(b) *Blacks and Blues*. These colours are on the increase, and seem at present to be coming through very well, although if carelessly bred with fawns this will eventually show.

There are those who say that a black or blue which 'paled-off' like some fawns would not be allowed to win, but I do not think this case ever arises. The 'paling-off' is seen in even the darkest colour fawns, and would appear to be a genetical factor. Therefore, it would seem impossible for a blue or black Great Dane to appear so marked. In certain parts of the Continent, Mantle Blacks (i.e. blacks with flashy white markings) can be shown; in this country they are referred to as Magpie Blacks, and are not acceptable as a show colour.

In conclusion I would urge the breed enthusiast to judge each Great Dane as a 'whole', remembering that the perfect specimen is yet to be bred. There are certain cardinal faults which one would not want to perpetuate deliberately or have in one's strain, but it is essential to learn to evaluate one fault against another. Never make the mistake of being so absorbed in one facet of the breed, to the exclusion of all others, that you eventually 'throw the baby out with the bath water'.

5

Choosing and Rearing a Puppy

IT never ceases to amaze me that so many people go out and buy a puppy in a hurry. When one acquires a new dog, it is going to be one of the most important members of the family or household for the next ten or twelve years. Therefore, take time and care when purchasing and buy wisely.

So often I am asked, 'Where should I buy?', in which case I am always happy to advise and recommend to the best of my ability. Unfortunately the public is not safeguarded in any way, and there are many traps when answering the casual advertisement. Perhaps one day there will be a Dog Breeders' Union, or an approved list of reliable breeders; until then the public is always wide open to 'buying a pup'!

What is best to do in the meantime? Any of the breed specialist clubs will be able to recommend breeders from whom puppies can be purchased with confidence, and the Kennel Club is also most helpful in this respect. When buying a Great Dane or any other large breed, it is imperative to ensure that the puppy has been correctly reared. There is no more sorry or pathetic sight than a rickety Great Dane. Another advantage of buying from well-known breeders is that they have a reputation which they are proud of and wish to retain. They are only too anxious that their clients should be satisfied, and that the puppies they sell should grow to be a credit to all concerned.

Moreover, the experienced breeders know how to price their stock correctly according to merit. I have known puppies of 'pet standard' being sold by novice breeders as potential show animals for top prices. It is a sad state of affairs when this sort of thing happens, so often done in good faith by the breeder of the litter in question. I recently heard of a black bitch with white feet, white blaze on chest and ingrowing (entropion) eyelids being offered at forty guineas at the age of eight weeks. The market price would have been nearer half this sum, as a pet only. Also, it should be the breeder's responsibility to arrange for the ingrowing eyelids to be operated upon by a veterinary surgeon before selling. This is an hereditary fault, now fortunately becoming very rare, and an animal with such a defect should, in the interests of the breed, only be sold with Kennel Club endorsed papers marked: 'Progeny not eligible for registration.'

Having warned you of some of the pitfalls, I will asume that you have made a few tentative enquiries from several breeders. The thing to decide now is whether to have a dog or bitch. Nowadays people are more enlightened about keeping bitches, and bitch or dog puppies are equally easy to sell. Dogs are always much larger than bitches, being taller, bigger-boned and generally greater in size. Many people insist on having a Great Dane which is really 'great', and a dog fulfils this ambition better than a bitch. However, people will tell you that once you have kept a bitch, you will never go back to having a dog. A Great Dane bitch is still a big animal when compared with most breeds, and the final choice rests with you. Remember that with normal luck you will have your Great Dane for a number of years. Choose an animal which will give you great pleasure, and will also be pleasant to look at and live with.

Should one buy a show puppy or a pet puppy? As a long-term result of selective breeding, pet puppies are now becoming increasingly rare. Gone are the days when it was considered lucky to have two or three outstanding puppies in a litter; now the position is reversed, and it is far more usual to find litters which have 'even' puppies all through, just the occasional 'throw-out' or 'mis-mark' appearing once in a while.

Do not take your puppy home until he is eight weeks old. By this time he will have been wormed and properly weaned, and will be ready to go out into the world. Many puppies are extremely forward and ready to leave the mother at six weeks, but with a change of environment or a long journey a puppy of this age would be more likely to have a setback which could do him a great deal of harm.

What is a fair price to pay? Running a kennel of Great Danes is an extremely costly business, and you must also remember that you are buying from a breeder with many years of experience and achievement. Every true breeder is trying to make the next generation better than the last. Again, no one can sell you a puppy as a 'certain champion'; all they can do is sell an eight-week-old puppy with no outstanding faults, in good faith. So much can happen in the months between puppyhood and adulthood that one must consider this partly a gamble.

At present market value I would consider about £225 a fair price to pay for a well-bred, well-reared pup. Prices can, of course, go higher, but sometimes a breeder has a hunch about a puppy and no amount of money will induce him to part with it in this case.

If possible, go to see the litter when they are about six weeks old; you will probably see several which catch your eye. Look for a well-balanced, sturdy puppy, with good broad hindquarters. The head should be square in appearance, and well filled in under the eyes which should be dark. The mouth should be correct, and at this age I prefer the top teeth to just overlap the bottom row (scissor bite). A level (pincher) bite, while acceptable in the breed, is not desirable in a young puppy, for the chances are that a mouth like this will 'go' and become undershot, which is considered by most judges to be a serious fault.

The puppies should be nicely covered without being too fat, and should feel firm and hard when handled; they should have fine, thick, 'tree-trunk' legs. You will notice the huge knobbly knees and elbows: unfortunately some veterinary surgeons not particularly familiar with puppies of large breeds have been known to become alarmed at the big knobbly limbs seen in young Danes. However, if they were not like that at an early age, they would be lacking in bone and would grow into light, spindly specimens. Provided the puppies are not splayed on their fronts, or cow-hocked behind, there is nothing to worry about.

A diet sheet is often supplied when you buy your puppy, but it is surprising how many of our successful breeders have quite different opinions on rearing; however, all end up with the same good results, so in the main, follow the diet sheet you are given.

You must remember that your puppy's rate of growth is going to be tremendous. There will be a time in his life when he grows at the rate of an inch a week, and puts on half a pound of weight a day. Common sense says that during this vital stage it is imperative to feed good, body-building food. Good food, little and often, should be the order of the day. Your pup is going to make his bone in the amazingly short time of five to six months, but he will continue to grow in height and generally fill out long after this. He will require at least four meals per day:

8 a.m.   Milk fortified with Farex.
12 noon 8 oz of raw meat, mixed with good quality puppy
         biscuit and a little stock.
4 p.m.   Similar to first feed. Add a raw egg-yolk.
8 p.m.   Similar to second meal. Add vitamins.
(This must be increased accordingly with age.)

Fresh water should always be available. Marrow bones, sawn into three, should also be regularly included, plus the large dog biscuits which are made by a number of leading biscuit manufacturers.

Feed a well-balanced diet of milk, meat and good-quality dog biscuit, and you should find that your puppy will do well. As he grows older, gradually decrease the number of meals but increase the quantity of food.

There are various vitamins available. We still prefer to feed bonemeal and cod-liver oil, and although considered old-fashioned by some breeders vitamins in this form are easily assimilated by dogs. Many of the new patent products now on the market can also be recommended. A sprinkling of seaweed powder on the food is, in my opinion, a 'must' for both the young and older dog. The growing puppy will require 1 tablespoon of bonemeal and a quarter-teaspoon of cod-liver oil. It is important not to feed several different vitamins, for there is a danger of upsetting the ratio.

Having arrived home with the apple of your eye, the next

Ch. Elch Edler of Ouborough

Ch. Challenger of Clausentum

Thomas A. Wilkie

Ch. Benign of Blendon

John Hopwood

Ch. Telaman of Moonsfield

Aus. Ch. Otto of Clausentum

Ch. Walkmyll Kaster of Clausentum

Diane Pearce

Ch. Clausentum Fenton of Fenbridge

Ch. Bencaross Beau Brummel

thing to consider is the best way to house it. Danes love companionship, and if you have one dog the place for it is undoubtedly in the home where it will be a delight to the family to whom it belongs. Start the new puppy in the kitchen, for it is unwise for him to have the run of the home until house-trained. Puppies love to be snug, and a wooden box with an old blanket or sweater is much preferred to a large basket or bed.

On the first night at home, give him a stone hot-water bottle. Many breeders also advise a ticking clock; its movement is said to comfort the puppy, for he thinks it is his mother's heart beating. You must turn a deaf ear to any cries, for if you once allow him into the bedroom he will be there for the rest of his life, and a Great Dane wanting to lie on top of your bed can become rather a problem, especially as he eventually weighs around 200 lb!

A puppy is easy to house-train. Let him out first thing in the morning, and of course last thing at night, and always immediately after he has had a meal or woken up. In the summer weather it is simple to leave the back door open so that he can run in and out of the kitchen as he pleases, and in this way you will find with luck that you have a house-trained dog within a few days. The early part of his life will be spent in eating, sleeping and growing, with romps around the garden as he feels in the mood.

Teach your puppy to become accustomed to being left on his own for short periods, so that later on you will have a dog you can confidently leave while out shopping or at a social function. It is surprising how many people one meets with various breeds, who are never able to spend an evening out 'because the dog will not be left'! Remember you want to have a dog which is a pleasure and a joy to own, and as the owner the final result is up to you. In the main, dogs reflect the personalities of their owners, so when you look at your pal dog it is rather like looking at yourself in a mirror!

Do have your puppy inoculated against hardpad and distemper. Most veterinary surgeons suggest eight to twelve weeks as a good age to commence these injections. In the meantime he can be protected with a temporary inoculation which gives immediate protection and is to be highly recommended. When it is time for the inoculations, make sure that your vet is going to use one of the prescribed vaccines produced in this country; some vets are now using the foreign vaccines, but we strongly advise the English inoculations which are specially prepared for the particular strains of virus which exist in this country.

Until the inoculations are fully completed—about a month— keep your dog in the garden and do not allow him to mix with strange dogs. In the meantime you can begin some early training; accustom him to a lightweight collar from the start. When you first introduce him to the lead, make a game of it, and if he pulls and bucks away, let the lead drop and go with him: don't pull him towards you. A few minutes spent on this each day, and you will soon have a 'lead-trained' dog.

Take him to any local obedience classes too. Here he will not only learn how to come when called, and not to pull on the lead, but will also be taught how to socialise with other dogs large and small, which is a very important part of his upbringing. Most large towns and cities run obedience training classes, and par-ticulars can be obtained from the Kennel Club. A few weeks' attendance will probably be sufficient, for in this time you and your dog will learn the rudimentary details of his good behaviour. I do not like an over-trained dog myself, but if you are 'bitten by the bug' you may decide to proceed to advanced training and obedience competition work.

The first few months of your dog's life will be fairly expensive. This is the time when you are building for the future, so your present outlay will be more than repaid when you finally have a dog to be proud of and which you can enjoy for a long time. The adult dog need not be too expensive for the average person to keep, allowing for the fact that any large breed costs more to maintain than a small variety. An adult Great Dane should cost no more per week than an average Boxer or Alsatian. £3.50 to £5·00 weekly is a fair sum to quote, and when one considers that this is less than the outlay on a packet of cigarettes each day, it is a small price to pay for the companionship and protection of a wonderful guard like a Great Dane.

When I was judging in America I was very impressed with their Danes, which are much bigger-bodied than the animals we have in this country. For an adult dog which is not being bred from, they suggest that 1 lb of meat daily (with added biscuit meal) is quite sufficient. In this country we have always tended to think of the Dane as a great meat-eater, although in the past I have advocated less meat for the grown animal. A dog fed mainly on a meat diet—although probably very fit—does not carry enough condition, and is often quite like a horse fed on too many oats—brimming over with energy.

At one time it was generally considered unwise to feed dog biscuit unless it was well soaked in either water or stock. New theories which have been brought forward rather dispel this idea, for food which has been soaked is far more likely to go sour, and could well account for stomach disorders. Police and Army dogs, which have to be kept in the peak of condition, have their meat rations with their kibbled biscuit dry to eat as they please. I mention this here because—like some other breeds—Great Danes suffer from flatulence, which can prove fatal; although, for the number of Danes bred, I would say the percentage of cases of distension is correspondingly low. Most breeders have lost one or two dogs with distension, but as they normally keep between twelve and twenty-four adult dogs in their kennels, I no longer accept that we should look upon this ailment as any more of a menace to our breed than bone cancer. But I will deal more fully with ailments in Chapter 11.

Take your puppy for short walks and let him meet people, particularly in crowds. As he grows older, take him for longer walks, but even with an adult Dane a couple of half-hourly trots a day plus a gallop in a nearby field or park will be sufficient for his requirements.

In addition to the good feeding which keeps your dog's coat in top condition, another essential is regular daily grooming. Since the Great Dane is a short-coated dog, he is an easy breed to keep clean, and his short coat also makes him free from the 'doggy' smell which is noticeable with the heavier-coated animals. The very action of the grooming stimulates the skin and sends the blood coursing round, and is vital to the well-being of the dog. In many kennels grooming is not accorded the importance it deserves, but in racing greyhound kennels it is considered an imperative part of the healthy animal's daily routine. Watch a bitch with her young litter and see how frequently she washes and licks the puppies; this is nature's way of stimulating them and generally toning them up. Just as fresh air is essential to the dog, grooming also plays an important part in contributing towards good overall condition.

Some people groom short-coated dogs by hand, using a method similar to that employed by the Arabs for their horses. The hair is raked up the wrong way for several minutes with a brisk action of the fingers, then finally finished off by smoothing down the coat with the flat of the palms of the hands (which can be dampened in order to remove any grease which may be on the coat).

There are some good hound gloves on the market, but do not use the wire type for they can so easily scratch the dog's skin and set up an irritation. The small rubber curry comb is also first class, and is about the best that one can use for a short-coated breed. The coat can be finished off with a light brush-down with a chamois leather, which will leave it glossy and bright.

Good feeding and a little time and care given to your dog will more than repay you in a fine, healthy Great Dane.

6

Establishing a Kennel and a Strain. Colours

To establish a kennel is one thing, but to establish a strain is quite another. When using the word 'establish' I feel it means more than just to set up a kennel. It also involves gaining a name and reputation which is going to be worth while in the breed of Great Danes, and eventually in the world of 'dogdom'.

However, it is always best to begin at the beginning. Very few breeders of dogs have started off by saying 'I am going to breed dogs'—it just doesn't seem to happen that way. The more usual process is that one buys a puppy with the object of acquiring a guard and companion. Then someone says 'you have a nice puppy there', and the whole thing commences from here. Most of today's famous breeders became bitten by the proverbial bug because they won a prize at a small show with their pal Dane.

When you have decided that you intend to breed Great Danes, there are a few essential points to bear in mind: firstly, that the most successful people are those who manage to restrict the number of inmates in their kennel. So many times I have seen how new enthusiasts to the breed can be quite carried away by their fresh interest, buying here and there in their anxiety to have the best winning dogs. Result—they all too quickly find themselves saddled with a mass of second-rate dogs. Then they discover that they have not got suitable facilities for housing their newly acquired animals, and that the dogs and bitches which were all the best of friends suddenly take violent dislikes to each other, and there are repeated nerve-racking fights. This is taking a dismal view of the unhappy experiences which newcomers may have when entering into the dog game, but I have seen similar situations arise all too often. The golden rule is never to overload yourself with dogs—it is far better to 'do' a few Great Danes really well.

Danes tend to thrive better in small numbers, and the one-dog owner with a really good animal is at a great advantage (although he does not always appreciate this at the time) over the so-called 'big' breeders. Your dogs will also emerge as much better animals if you can give them plenty of time—time to know and treat them individually, time to give them their daily controlled exercises, and time to groom them and attend to the many other daily chores.

First of all, acquire one or two good bitches. Never buy a dog unless you are fortunate enough to be able to purchase a top-class, show male. If you have some nicely bred bitches as your nucleus, then you will have the choice of all the best stud dogs in the country, and this is far the best way to set out on the path to successful breeding. Study the various blood-lines, go to as many shows as you can, and make up your own mind as to what is the correct type to breed for. Acquaint yourself also with the background of as many strains as possible, and make sure that they are free from serious hereditary faults.

Besides being well bred, your foundation bitches must also be free from constructional faults. Excellent temperaments are of paramount importance, for no animal—however beautiful—can be an asset to its breed if it has an unsound temperament. Without these basic essentials you will be commencing on a course which can never bring worthwhile results.

The establishment of a strain takes a very long time. A breeder becomes known for producing a particular type, and then through line-breeding and in-breeding establishes a family like-ness which is recognisable anywhere. This can only be done over several generations, and a breeder cannot fairly be said to have produced a strain until he or she has at least three generations of their own breeding on both sides of the pedigree.

Occasionally a breeder will out-cross to another line, but the puppies he will finally select and keep are bound to be those which resemble his own stock, and which he quite naturally prefers. Consequently these puppies, when adult and bred from and mated back into the previously established strain, tend to strengthen the original strain still further.

The ideal method is to line-breed. Now and again a breed will produce a great animal; a dog or bitch of this calibre is quickly recognised and appreciated by those who know, and efforts are then made to line up to it on as many occasions as possible.

A dog which readily comes to mind is the post-war champion Elch Edler of Ouborough. He was probably the greatest specimen to appear in the breed after the war, and his win of Supreme Champion at Cruft's—the largest dog show in the world—in 1954 has not been equalled before or since by any other Great Dane. At that time the breed was not as popular as it is today, and Ch. Elch Edler was not widely used at stud. Nevertheless, he had a tremendous impact on the breed, and I think it would be safe to say that there is not a fawn or brindle in the country today which does not carry at least one line back to him; in fact, many of our top winners have as many as six lines to this particular dog. This is the essence of line-breeding.

In-breeding is mating half-brother to sister, brother to sister, mother to son, father to daughter and so on—not to be recommended unless you are dealing with really great animals. This type of breeding can perpetuate the faults besides stamping the virtues, and a breeder can only too soon find himself at a 'point of no return'.

There are exceptions to all rules, and probably more so in livestock breeding, which is extremely unpredictable. In certain cases, clever in-breeding has produced fantastic animals, but this process is like playing with fire and should always be left to the experts. To practise breeding as close as this, it is essential to have a full and detailed knowledge of the forbears.

With close breeding always be prepared to dispose of the stock which does not measure up to your standard as 'pets only'.

Then there is out-cross mating. The old adage tells us that like begets like, but all kennels should periodically bring new blood into their line, for too much breeding back into one's own line causes reduction of size and bone and eventually loss of fertility. Ideally, the out-cross dog should himself come from a first-class strain which is line-bred; an out-cross mating can be like a breath of fresh air to an old strain.

All strains have certain weaknesses, although some breeders would be loth to admit it. Therefore if your animals have predominantly light eyes, long backs or straight stifle, make doubly sure that the stud dog you use has none of these faults himself or immediately behind him.

Sadly, one so often sees breeders forming themselves into little camps favouring their various types. Then along comes a newcomer who is not influenced by the differing schools of thought; he decides for himself the course his breeding programme will take, blends two famous lines together, and—hey presto!— breeds dogs better than anyone else. This is grand when it happens, but the snag which then arises is 'Where do we go from here?' How often has a newcomer bred a great dog, and then found he is in 'the middle of the road'. The real test comes when it is a question of whether he can breed another dog of equal merit, or can produce better stock on the second and subsequent generations.

So often the novice reaches the heights, only to find that he has not the 'knack', 'know-how', 'gift'—call it what you will—to progress. Here the wise and experienced breeders are at an advantage, for although they may have had their ups and downs from time to time, they have learned the hard way, and know that however much is written or said about dog breeding, it can never become a science and will always remain a challenge.

For my part, I look upon dog breeding as rather like a game of chance depending upon the throw of a dice. Sometimes one may be lucky and get all sixes. However, the sixes must be there in the first place in order to have a chance to come up, and this may well account for the cases where repeat matings quite often produce different results.

COLOURS

There are five recognised colours—harlequins, blacks, blues, fawns and brindles. Now it is best to decide which colours you will concentrate on right from the outset. I am afraid the lady who wrote to me from South Africa saying she wished to import a male harlequin and a brindle bitch as a breeding pair because she was 'interested to breed all the recognised colours' would have been greatly disappointed with the resultant puppies if she ever bred from a pair such as this.

Of all the colours the harlequin is the most difficult to breed, and so often it has been referred to as the hobby of millionaires. I do not altogether agree with this view, however, for over the years successful breeders of this rare and beautiful variety of Great Dane seem to have had a flare or hunch for producing the harlequin.

Wealthy people have taken up the breeding of this most difficult of colours, and with a comparatively small financial outlay they have achieved wonderful results. The heartbreaking thing about breeding harlequins is that the mating of two wonderful specimens can result in a litter of mis-marks: merles (which are not recognised), blacks with too much white and very heavily marked harlequins are all too frequently the products of harlequin-harlequin mating.

The harlequin is a specialised taste and a beautiful variety of Great Dane, but its rarity makes it hard to obtain and highly prized and priced when available. The very variety gives an unscrupulous breeder an opportunity to take unfair advantage of potential buyers. A really well-marked harlequin, and I emphasise the word 'well', is worth a very good price indeed, but a poorly marked specimen is in a different category altogether and should be priced substantially lower.

There is a tendency to think that blues and blacks belong to the same family, but the harlequin-bred black can appear and be extremely useful for breeding harlequins. Blacks which are not related to the harlequins should not at any time be crossed with this colour. Blues and blacks are from time to time brought into the fawn and brindle line, but this is done more in the way of an experiment and should be left to the experts. The fawn and brindle family are the same, and should not at any time be crossed with harlequins.

There are those who maintain that the blues and blacks should be kept as separate families too, and I must say that I rather go along with this theory. Not until after the war was colour crossing permitted to any degree by the established breeders, and then it was mainly from necessity rather than choice. At that time the blues were practically extinct, and the blacks very rare, so that the only way open to breeders if they wanted to save and improve the quality of these two colours was to introduce fawn and brindle blood.

This has been done with excellent results for the blues and blacks, and they have now reached a stage where they are feeling the full benefit of the influence of the fawn and brindle blood-lines.

I feel that the blues and blacks, however, have little to offer to the already strong family of fawns and brindles, and it would be a great pity if the fawn and brindle breeders made a common practice of crossing blues and blacks into their lines. In the end it could well be to the detriment of all these colours which—other than the harlequin which is a law unto itself—if properly selected will always breed true.

With the increasing popularity of the breed, blue fawns and rusty blacks have been seen far too often and there is no need whatsoever for this.

7

Breeding a Litter

THE utmost care should always be taken when selecting a suitable
stud dog for your bitch. How often does one hear someone say,
'I just wanted the bitch to have puppies for *her* sake'! Or 'My
friend, who has a Great Dane, thought it would be a good idea
if I mated my bitch to his dog.' What one would really like to hear
more often is, 'I am thinking of breeding a litter from my bitch,
and I am anxious to do the best I possibly can for the breed.'

Breeding livestock should always be a matter for careful
consideration. Be prepared to travel *any* distance in order to use
what you consider is the right stud dog for your bitch. All
breeders should have uppermost in their minds the arrangement
of a mating which they feel will be doing a service to the breed,
and not—as so often happens—a disservice to the Great Dane.
An ill-chosen stud dog can not only put back the breeder for
years but sometimes even harm the breed itself.

How does one find the right dog? Out of many considerations,
the paramount. one should always be temperament, and all
breeders could well have as their motto, 'temperament before all
else'. Without good temperament a dog is nothing, for what is
the point of having the most beautiful dog in the world if it is
afraid of its own shadow? Select, therefore, a dog which pleases
you with his gay, bold, yet kindly disposition. Remember too that
if you want to breed dogs you are thereby assuming a certain
responsibility, and your prime wish should always be for the
betterment of the breed. The puppies you are eventually going to
breed, rear and sell should go out into the world as a credit to
both you and the Great Dane breed which they represent.

Always use the best stud dogs. I was tempted to say use only the best you are able to afford, but this should not apply when breeding. If you are unable to view cost as very much a secondary consideration when choosing your stud dog and rearing your puppies, then it would be better not to breed at all. Trying to cut costs will prove to be false economy in the long run, for there is always a market for really well-bred, well-reared puppies. Successful breeding is an extremely costly matter, and few of our well-known breeders are lucky to break even after all their expenses are paid. However, I will deal with costs in another chapter.

Choose a dog because *you* like him, and do not allow yourself to be influenced by other breeders when you finally make your decision; they will only too often point out the faults of a dog you admire, especially if it belongs to a rival kennel. Sad to say, few are generous in their appraisal of another breeder's dogs, although happily on rare occasions one meets a connoisseur of Great Danes who is in no way influenced by blood-lines, and will be only too pleased to give credit to a good Dane regardless of how or by whom he is bred. In all fairness, one must admit that the perfect specimen has not yet been produced in any breed, but on rare occasions a lovely animal will come very near to the ideal standard, and when this happens he or she will be widely acclaimed.

However, one must not be too critical of the successful breeders who are anxious to tell you that their dogs are 'the best in the country'. One is reminded of the old adage that 'blood is thicker than water'; to some breeders—rather like mothers with their children—all their geese are swans, and they tend to see all their dogs through rose-coloured spectacles.

In choosing the stud dog, how important is the breeding behind him? This is a difficult question to answer, for ideally you want both—the good dog *and* the good pedigree. I have known of people using a mediocre dog because they like the way he is bred, but the fact remains that like begets like, and if one uses a poor type of dog because he is 'nicely bred' it should be logical that he then becomes part of the family tree, and his inferior influence may be evident in the second and subsequent generations.

Bad mouths (undershot jaws) are a good case in point, for this is a serious fault which is far too common in a breed which has been established for so many years. Breeders who have bred from dogs and bitches with such mouths will assure you that the resulting puppies 'all had perfect mouths', and this is probably quite true. However, it is the unsuspecting newcomer who eventually breeds from one of these puppies, without being fully aware of their background, who finds when he has a litter that the fault has suddenly appeared in a number of his puppies. Faults have a nasty habit of skipping a generation or two, and then reappearing with a vengeance. Furthermore, the newcomer may find himself doubling up on a fault, unless he has the good fortune to be well advised by a far-sighted expert on the breed.

Costs of keeping and showing a stud dog are high, and you will find that the usual fee asked may vary from £150 upwards. This is not so high as may at first appear, for your puppies will be carrying half his line. You may well be procuring a famous line which has taken a lifetime to build up, and has also cost a great deal of money in the process. Also, using a stud dog with a 'name' has its advantages, for the puppies will be in demand and sell well.

This brings me to another point. I feel that far too many small breeders (for want of a better word) keep their own stud dogs. Never keep a dog unless you rate him a potential champion, since he will be an added expense on your kennel account, and barely worth his keep. It is interesting to note that some of our most successful breeders have been those who have gone outside their own kennels and used the top stud dogs, thus building up a strong line of bitches, and then waiting until they too breed a dog puppy which they can truthfully say is 'out of the top drawer'.

I am frequently asked by owners of one dog if they should put him at stud. If he is an exceptionally good animal, likely to reach the top in the show ring, my answer would be, 'Yes, every time'. But if he is foremost your companion and guard do think carefully before allowing him to be used at stud. A stud dog can become aggressive towards other male dogs, and while this is not an unnatural state of affairs when one considers that in his wild state he would probably want to be the 'boss' dog of the pack, it has distinct disadvantages if he is primarily your companion, pet and house guard.

When you have finally selected the dog you wish to use, inform the owner that you would like to bring your bitch to their stud dog. Owners of stud dogs reserve the right to refuse bitches, and it is for this reason that you will read on the stud card 'to approved bitches only'. However, this is merely a safeguard, and in fact a bitch is seldom refused. The stud owner will require to know in good time when your bitch is in season, and to arrange a suitable date for the mating. It is useless to telephone the day before, for it is highly probable that the dog has been already booked for another bitch.

The bitch will be in season for twenty-one days, and the first day of her season should be counted from the day on which she first shows colour. The best time to mate her is on the eleventh to thirteenth day, and from experience we now find the thirteenth day ideal. A bitch which is mated too early or too late in her season may not be ovulating, and if this is the case the mating will not of course be effective and the bitch will not 'take'.

Should your bitch miss to the dog, the owner will probably offer you one free service when she next comes into season. There is no obligation to do so, but it is an unwritten law which is generally accepted throughout the dog world. Do check this point at the time so that there is no possibility of a future misunderstanding.

Now to consider the brood bitch, for it has often been said that the strength of a breed lies in its bitches. Undoubtedly the good brood bitch is worth a fortune, and it is strange that bitches which have never made much of an impression in the show ring have repeatedly produced top-quality puppies. An analysis of these bitches usually reveals that they are what I call good honest animals with no outstanding faults. They must be well balanced, sound and without structural faults, but if perhaps they lack a little 'showiness' this does not matter. I must emphasise here that I do not think a poor type of bitch is going to breed good puppies, any more than a second-rate stud dog.

Obtain a good opinion of your bitch. The best way is to show a few times under specialist and all-round judges, thereby getting a very good overall assessment. Do not breed from her if she is nervous or badly constructed; keep her as a pet and buy a more suitable animal.

With breeding one should always be selective and aim only for the highest standard. It is seldom possible to reach the heights for which one aims, but set your sights high, for if you only aspire to a medium standard, you may fall short even of this.

Never before in the history of 'dogdom' have newcomers been at such an advantage. If they so decide they can purchase the best, and then have the choice of the top stud dogs in the country. It is sometimes possible to purchase a brood bitch, but on the whole they are extremely rare. A breeder cannot easily price a good breeding bitch, for if he takes into consideration the fact that she might produce several more litters, this would put her at a near prohibitive price. On rare occasions a breeder who is overstocked may agree to let an older bitch go out on part-time breeding terms, and this can be an excellent way of procuring a first-class foundation for a kennel.

The general care of the stud dog and brood bitch are similar: good, dry, draught-free kennelling, with ample light and fresh air, which, supplemented by a sensible and well-balanced diet, should keep the animals in excellent health.

When the brood bitch has been mated, she should have extra meat and milk added to her diet, and also an occasional raw egg. Right from the start she should also be given vitamins such as bonemeal, calcium, cod-liver oil or any one of the specially balanced preparations which are now on the market. It is important not to feed several of these various vitamins at once, for the ratio can be upset and they will then do more harm than good. If in doubt, consult your vet.

Exercise your mated bitch in the usual way, and keep her in fit, strong condition. Bitches which are flabby and in soft condition produce more whelping problems, so a regular daily gallop plus some road walking exercise should keep her in good trim. When she is obviously showing in whelp, let her take things a little more easily, and cut out galloping and running loose with other dogs. When she is seven weeks in whelp, introduce her to the kennel where she will have her puppies. This should be roomy and large enough for her to move around, an ideal size

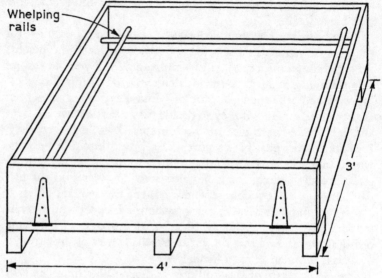

Whelping rails

FIG. 14 Whelping box (minimum size)

being a shed about 8 × 8 ft. square. The shed should contain a whelping box which can be specially made by a carpenter (see Fig. 14); it should measure about 4 × 3 ft. and be fitted with a drop front. The fixing of a guard rail—similar to a farrowing rail used for pigs—is absolutely essential. Should the bitch push a puppy against the side of the box, the puppy cannot be crushed, for it will slide very conveniently under the protective rail.

An infra-red lamp should be safely fixed over the whelping box and tested for heat in order to ensure that the temperature is about 70°F. It is important that the bitch should not be too hot, and that later on the puppies themselves should not be subjected to over-heating. These lamps are ideal, and have definitely helped to decrease the mortality rate among puppies.

The bitch should be well bedded on wood wool or clean wood shavings. Do not use straw, for as I have mentioned in another chapter, it has many disadvantages. By the time the bitch is due to whelp, she should be thoroughly happy and accustomed to her new quarters. Have plenty of newspapers handy as well, for these are very useful when she is actually whelping. Newspapers are antiseptic, and by this stage the wood shavings should have been removed and the bitch bedded on the newspapers, which can easily be replaced whenever necessary.

The usual period of gestation is sixty-three days, although it is not uncommon for a bitch to whelp a couple of days either side of the due date. Some will produce as much as five days before their time, but one hopes that this will not occur, for the puppies may not then be so robust as those born on the sixty-third day or later.

When the bitch is about to whelp she quite often refuses her food and becomes restless, and her temperature falls. She then begins to tear up her bed, and it should not be long after this that the first puppy appears. Most bitches like to have someone with them, although they do not want a crowd and prefer comparative quietness. With luck your bitch will have her puppies quite easily, and know exactly what to do—breaking the bag, severing the cord and then cleaning each puppy up. The pups will probably be strong, and before many minutes have passed, will be round feeding at the 'milk bar'.

If you are not quite so lucky, you may find that your bitch needs a little help. Have at hand a *blunt* pair of sterilised scissors, and be ready to break the bag and cut the cord several inches from the puppy.

It is ideal if the bitch has her puppies at fairly frequent intervals, perhaps every half-hour. Sometimes there may be longer intervals than this, but if there is some delay do not hesitate to call in your veterinary surgeon, who will have various ways of speeding things up. The great danger is that if she is allowed to wait around too long between having each puppy, she is of course becoming weaker all the time and 'inertia' sets in. Should it be necessary for her to have a caesarian section, it is important that her strength has been maintained; many bitches have been lost when having caesarians because the operation has been left too late. One naturally prefers to avoid a caesarian unless it is absolutely necessary, but the all-important time factor decides whether you can save your bitch, your puppies, or both.

Should your bitch go to her full sixty-three days and then

show no obvious signs of whelping, I think it is best to avoid taking any risks and have her checked over by the vet. He is then fully aware of the situation, and will probably ask you to keep in close touch with him, for it is unlikely that he will allow her to go more than two to three days longer without deciding on an operation.

Assuming there are no problems and the bitch is whelping normally, remain with her. If she has a weak puppy you may be able to revive it by briskly rubbing it in a clean towel and putting just the smallest drop of brandy on its tongue. Have a cardboard carton on one side, and then if there are a large number of puppies you can remove several (make sure they are kept warm) while she is busy coping with the others. In the case of a large litter the earlier puppies can get in the bitch's way and be easily crushed, so removing some of them temporarily obviates this danger. In between each birth you can give her a short walk—only a minute or so—but take great care to see that she does not drop a puppy or get cold.

When you think she has completed whelping—the discharge usually turns from green to brown at this stage—ask your vet to look in and give her a final check over. He will probably also give her a penicillin injection to reduce any risk of infection, and confirm that there are no more pups left behind to cause trouble.

Feed her mainly on fluids for the next thirty-six hours, and then gradually bring her back to a normal diet with plenty of meat. Remember that meat makes milk, and that during the next few weeks she will be extremely busy looking after her valuable puppies.

You should also check that the puppies are suckling properly and all getting sufficient milk. It is a sensible precaution to watch both puppies and bitch closely for a few days, for sometimes the milk does not come down properly, or else you may have 'fading' puppies. Your vet will attend to both these worries, and in cases where a bitch has insufficient milk there are sometimes injections which will remedy matters. On very rare occasions the bitch may not have any milk at all, but in normal circumstances the milk usually comes down once the puppies start to feed, even if it takes a day or two to do so.

Unfortunately little is known about 'fading', a condition which sometimes affects puppies within twenty-four hours of birth. They normally appear to be beautiful at birth, and very strong, but for some unaccountable reason fail to thrive, lose ground rapidly and invariably die. Fading puppies are usually quite easy to spot because they are not contented, continually cry and do not seem to make any progress. We have found that two or three drops of intramammary terramycin given to all the puppies, twice a day for at least three days, seems to obviate this worry; in fact, we have not had a fading puppy for years now, and attribute it mainly to the use of this antibiotic.

As a routine, always feel your bitches' glands several times a day to see that they are quite soft and free from any hard lumps. Mastitis can set in in a matter of a few hours, and if not attended to immediately you may have a very sick bitch on your hands and find it necessary to hand-rear her puppies.

The next important thing to arrange with your vet is for the removal of the puppies' dew claws. These are small extra claws (rather like thumbs) found always on the front legs and sometimes on the back, and are best removed because they are not only unsightly but tend to become caught in things as the dog gets older, and can be a general nuisance. It is ideal if they are removed at about four days, by which time the puppies should have a substantial hold on life.

Arrange to take several of the puppies away—the remainder being left with the bitch—while the vet removes their dew claws, and also ensure that their cries are well out of earshot of their dam. Do not forget to check again for back dew claws, though these are now rare. Make quite sure that none of the puppies is bleeding, and then return them to their mother before collecting the others so that their dew claws can be removed in turn.

Keep the puppies on thick newspaper for several days, and then bed them down nicely on wood shavings or wood wool just as the mother had prior to whelping. Make the usual routine checks to ensure that the bitch is well and eating correctly, and that the puppies are feeding and growing as they should be.

The colours of the puppies will be easily recognisable at this stage. The fawns will be beige, with a thick donkey stripe down the back; some will have much black about the mask and ears, and the darker they are when born the richer the final colouring will be. The brindles are easy to spot, as right from birth the stripes are clearly defined; here again some may appear darker than others, and this will distinguish between the darker- and lighter-coloured animals.

You may find that some of the pups have white on their toes when born, and also white on their chests; this is nothing to worry about, for it lessens as the puppy grows and quite often disappears altogether. Occasionally one sees a puppy with a white blaze on the throat—as distinct from white on the chest—and the chances are that it will end up as a mis-mark. Sometimes a puppy with a white sock, or even a white stocking, will appear; this is a definite colour fault, and a puppy so marked should be sold as 'a pet only' with endorsed Kennel Club papers or no pedigree. Animals such as this should not be bred from.

Harlequins, blacks and blues are also easily identifiable when first born. Harlequins frequently have all-pink noses, but provided there is a pinpoint of black it is fairly certain that the nose will completely fill in with black before the dog is eighteen months old. The standard allows 'butterfly noses' in this colour, and I have elaborated on this more fully in Chapter 5 when dealing with breed standards in general.

Some blues and blacks have a little white on toes and chest, but this is not in any way serious. On the other hand, blacks should *be* black and blues blue, for a rusty tinge about either (other than when the adult dog is moulting) is incorrect.

It may be appropriate to mention here the various colours which can be crossed. In this country we are more inclined to be lax in colour breeding than other nations, but I am not prepared to say whether we are right or wrong. On the credit side is the fact that when blacks and blues have been crossed into the brindle and fawn lines, this has been to the advantage of the former colours, since their overall standard (until recently below that of the other colours) has been improved by the quality of the fawns and brindles. However, I would also say that the disadvantage of crossing these colours is that we inevitably have a number of blacks with a fawn tinge and fawns which have a blue look about them: in other words, rusty blacks and blue fawns.

When this happens it is a great pity, and those who knowingly breed these undesirable colours have not the true interests of the breed at heart.

We can be certain that fawn mated to fawn will always breed true, and fawn puppies will result. Fawn bred to brindle or vice versa will sometimes give both fawns and brindles in one litter, although it can equally well produce all fawns or all brindles. A brindle to brindle mating—seldom done—can produce fawns or brindles, but such a mating is not popular since it tends to result in brindle puppies which are too dark to be desirable. Some years ago, I saw a litter of puppies from a brindle to brindle mating, and they were so dark that it was questionable whether the stripes were 'clearly defined' according to the standard definition.

At one time I felt it was necessary to bring a brindle into one's breeding plan fairly frequently, but experience has proved that provided the fawns carry good colours, fawn to fawn matings can be practised for several generations without any deterioration in colouring or pigmentation.

The Americans are very strict about the colour problem, and to become a member of the Great Dane Club of America the following code of ethics must be adhered to:

THE GREAT DANE CLUB OF AMERICA

Color classifications being well founded, The Great Dane Club of America, Inc., considers it an inadvisable practice to mix color strains, and it is the Club's policy to adhere only to the following matings:

FAWN bred to FAWN or BRINDLE

BRINDLE bred to FAWN or BRINDLE

HARLEQUIN bred to HARLEQUIN or BLACK

BLACK bred to HARLEQUIN, BLUE or BLACK

BLUE bred to BLUE or BLACK

It is our belief that color mixing other than that set forth above is injurious to our breed especially in the third, fourth and later generations.

The Great Dane Club of America, Inc.

Some American breeders with whom I have discussed this say that colour influence can still come through after fifteen generations.

Ideally, I feel that when those who are interested in the various colours have achieved a certain standard of merit, it is then desirable not to cross the colours more than is absolutely necessary. Therefore, the ideal colour breeding pattern to follow is that already put forward by the Great Dane Club of America, who have done a great deal of research into this.

When the puppies are about three weeks old, arrange for them to have some finely scraped or minced beef, offering a very small amount in the palm of the hand to each individual pup. At this age also make sure that their nails have been cut back on to the quick, for if this is not attended to they can claw and scratch the mother and cause her a great deal of distress.

The daily progress the puppies make at this stage is amazing. By the time they are four weeks old they should also be having some milk or one of the many recommended milk foods which are now available on the dog market. Supplement this with Farex or something similar; as a guide, four tablespoons of Farex, etc., to one pint of milk makes a very good consistency. Gradually step up the number of meals until at six weeks they are having five small meals each day; many breeders have different ideas, but the basic principle is good food little and often. A rough guide is given below:

1st Meal Milk fortified with Farex, and a raw egg yolk.

2nd Meal Raw chopped meat. If desired, supplement two-thirds of raw tripe with one-third of raw meat. Good quality puppy meal. Feed fairly dry, but the food may be dampened with a little good quality stock.

3rd Meal Another milk meal similar to the first, but without the egg yolk.

4th Meal Similar to the second.

5th Meal Similar to the first, with a few hard biscuits for chewing.

At one of these meals—preferably the second—add the various

vitamins which are essential for puppies of this age. For example, we would give a six-week-old Great Dane puppy a dessertspoon of bonemeal, a teaspoon of seaweed powder, and a quarter teaspoon of cod-liver oil each day. This would be substantially increased as the puppy grows older; do not increase the cod-liver oil, however, because attention has recently been drawn to the fact that it is possible to overdose on vitamin D which it contains. On the other hand, the dog cannot assimilate the bonemeal without also having vitamin D.

As I have mentioned previously, there is always a danger of upsetting the balance of vitamins, so do not think that because a certain amount of one thing is good for a dog, double the quantity is necessarily twice as good. It has been proved that although puppies receiving insufficient vitamins will have rickets, a rickety condition can also result from an imbalance or overdose of vitamins. Consult your vet if you have the slightest worry over this—he has up-to-date ideas on all these subjects.

If the puppies have been properly weaned by the time they are eight weeks of age they can be brought down on to four meals a day in accordance with the particulars given in Chapter 5.

To revert to the puppies at four weeks of age, worming has advanced over the past few years and is now a comparatively safe and easy process. All puppies have worms, and some are literally stuffed with them, so do not be worried if your puppies pass masses of them when wormed. With improved modern methods, worm your puppies for the first time at four weeks, for the sooner they are rid of these pests the more progress they are going to make. As a matter of fact, I find that after worming they go ahead in leaps and bounds. Worm for the second time ten days later.

Your veterinary surgeon (or Boots or any good chemist) will supply you with Antoban tablets which require no dieting and are straightforward to use. Being non-toxic (the worms are paralysed), they are quite harmless to the dog, and in the case of young Great Dane puppies it is a good idea to worm regularly once a month until they are six months old, thus ensuring that there is no retardation at this most important stage in the animals' growth. At one time there was a real fear attached to worming and a certain element of danger was involved, but due to the advancement of veterinary science this is no longer so.

Many breeders allow their puppies to be sold under eight weeks of age, but I believe this is wrong. At eight weeks or over, the young puppy is really established and ready to go out into the world, fully weaned, properly wormed and old enough to withstand any minor setback which a change of environment can sometimes cause.

When the puppies are about five weeks of age they may become too much for their mother. Arrange for her to be able to get away from them by giving her a high bench where she can sleep and not be bothered by her young ones. She may only wish to be with them for a short while, so that they can take off the milk which would otherwise cause her pain and distress.

If puppies are left with their dam for too long, they frequently spoil her undercarriage. In the case of the show bitch it is most important that this should not happen, and it can be avoided if she is removed from the puppies in good time. I have seen breeding bitches return to the show ring looking as though they have never even had a litter, whereas others have been quite spoiled. As I mentioned earlier, there is no need for this whatsoever, so make quite sure that by the time the puppies are eight weeks old they have been completely weaned off their mother.

If you want to do everything possible for your lovely puppies, you can now arrange to have them immunised when only a few weeks old with a temporary inoculation against hardpad and distemper. This expense can be added to the selling price of the puppy, and many new owners are extremely pleased to find that their dogs have been safeguarded in order to tide them over the danger period of a few weeks, until they are old enough to have their full, permanent inoculations.

To sum up, remember that dog breeding can never become computerised—the elements of luck and chance will always remain. However, if your sole interest is for the betterment of the breed, aim to be highly selective at all times. Do not keep a stud dog unless he is a top show animal who can not only be used by you for breeding, but will also be in demand by other breeders. Unless he is a dog of this calibre, he will not be worth his keep.

So far as the brood bitch is concerned, make sure that she has all the basic essentials required in a good dog. Do not make a machine of her—one litter a year is ample for your bitch to produce, and she should not be bred from for the first time until she is at least eighteen months old.

8

Housing and Kennelling

LET me say straight away that I do not recommend the one-dog owner to kennel his dog outside. Those who have had the good fortune to own a Great Dane realise that they are very special animals; a Dane owner rarely changes to another breed, for the pleasure and delight they give cannot be appreciated by those who have not kept one of these noble giants.

For his size, the Great Dane is a gentle dog, who tends to be 'toffee-nosed' with strangers but is always loyal and anxious to please his owner or family. He is a great guard also, but only seen in this light if really provoked, when he becomes a formidable adversary to say the least.

Kennelling a dog on his own is like sentencing a person to solitary confinement. And who wants to live a life of solitude? In spite of his size, the Great Dane takes up little room in the house, and his good manners—which seem to accord with his aristocratic breeding and noble bearing—tend to make him 'seen but not heard'. The one drawback to having him in the house is that on a cold winter's night you may have to view the fire from a distance! He can be a real hearthrug breed of dog, who enjoys his home comforts, but fortunately in this day of centrally heated houses this is not a problem to unduly disturb most households.

I would like to mention here that I feel the warm houses which we now seem to take for granted may account for so many breeds moulting at various times of the year. One now hears of dogs losing their coats at almost any season, and it could well be that the artificial heat has upset nature's normal cycle, for a dog usually casts his coat twice a year. The dog's coat can be kept in fine condition by a daily five-minute rub down with a hound brush, or even with one's own hand.

Assuming that your dog is living in the house, let him have the kitchen as his base, since it would not be wise to allow him the freedom of the whole house until he is house-trained and has outgrown his mischievous puppy ways. A young, healthy dog, rather like a high-spirited child, goes through stages when he almost drives his owners to distraction. These are just passing phases, and with a kind but firm upbringing he will grow into a sedate adult and be a pleasure to his owners. However, I would just point out here that the young Great Dane does need a certain amount of discipline if he is not to grow into a spoiled animal who is eventually a nuisance to his owners and their friends.

Arrange for your young Dane to start off in a small wooden box, which can easily be disposed of in favour of a bigger one as he rapidly grows. It is strange how dogs have a feeling of security if they have a box of their own to go to. See how the average dog will curl up in a small space or under the table, presumably feeling in some way protected.

Do not make the common mistake of buying a brand-new basket for your puppy. Besides unnecessary expense, it will not be appreciated in the least, or not in the way we would expect! Your young Dane will delight in picking it to pieces, and in a few weeks there will be little of your lovely dog basket left. A basket that can be chewed also represents a certain hazard, for there is always the danger that the puppy may swallow a piece which could be injurious to him or even cause death.

When he has got over the chewing stage, buy him one of the 'Safari'-type beds. These are really first class, and can be purchased from any good dog shop. Foam-rubber mattresses also make excellent dog beds, and it is a good plan to make several covers which can be frequently washed and changed with the minimum amount of fuss. However, do not introduce the foam-rubber bedding until you are quite sure that your Dane really has outgrown all his puppy ways, otherwise it will only be a short time before it is torn into a thousand pieces!

I am always surprised by the number of people who become worried when their puppy goes through the boisterous stage.

As with all breeds, this is just a normal part of growing up, and the strong healthy puppy is bound to be full of beans and up to all the tricks.

In the teething stage, which can last until eight months, you can help him a great deal by always seeing that he has a marrow bone available to chew on; ask your butcher to saw a large marrow bone into three, and this will keep the dog highly amused for hours. *Never* tease a dog with a bone, for even the best-tempered animals can be possessive over this, and never, of course, let several dogs have their bones together.

You may be told by some people that a dog's mouth can be spoiled by bones, that is to say it may become overshot or under-shot—both very serious faults. Others will tell you just the opposite, and say that allowing a puppy to have bones will keep a mouth correct. My own conclusion is that both these theories are wrong, since there is little doubt that these are hereditary faults which are likely to crop up in the breed from time to time. If a dog is going to end up with a good mouth, nothing will prevent it, but the reverse is also true: nothing can be done to help a dog destined to have a bad mouth, for good mouths are bred, not made.

It is important to remember that although the dog is domesticated, he should always be allowed to live as near to nature as his modern environment will permit. He does not chew and masticate his food as we do, and ideally his meat should be in large chunks. The gnawing of a bone serves many purposes, for besides keeping the teeth clean and free from tartar it also makes the digestive juices work. Indeed, one of the first things recommended for dogs which suffer from rickets is that they should have bones available to chew on as and when they want.

To sum up for the owner of a single pet dog, let him have the kitchen as his base, but allow him the run of the house in due course. *Always* have fresh water available.

Now for the enthusiast who is going to keep several Great Danes and breed them, and who will therefore be quartering them outside the house. They must of course be properly housed, as no dog will survive in damp or dark conditions, however well fed. Great Danes can be extremely tough and hardy if reared under and accustomed to a kennel environment, but a little common sense is always invaluable when planning the best kind of kennel to build. Naturally the type of kennels you wish to have must be controlled by whether you are a millionaire or a person who has a limited amount of cash to spend on your hobby of breeding these dogs.

If your kennels are to be built regardless of expense, then the dogs which are housed in them will indeed be lucky. I have seen beautifully designed kennels with double-cavity walls, under-floor heating and in fact all the facilities one would expect in any modern house. I have also seen brick-built accommodation which is damp and cold, and no amount of enthusiasm and goodwill will enable one to breed good dogs under these conditions.

I feel that old stables—frequently converted into kennels—so often fail in this respect, as they tend to be cold, damp and dark. Where old buildings are adapted, make sure that your dogs have plenty of air and light, with large wooden boxes well off the ground to protect them from draughts, and plenty of deep bedding. If old outbuildings are used for kennelling, they only seem to make satisfactory night quarters, and on the whole do not lend themselves for use as round-the-clock housing.

Visit a number of kennels before you finally draw up your plans, and pool the best of all the ideas. It is my opinion that timber kennelling still takes a lot of beating. The price is not usually so prohibitive, and the handyman can build his own kennels with some help. Have them raised well off the ground, so that they keep dry and do not attract rats.

It is wise to arrange for two Danes to share each kennel and run; if housed in larger groups, they may agree for a time, but when a fight does come it can be a most unpleasant experience. A practical point to bear in mind is that they are a short-coated breed; if they do become involved in a fight unsightly scars may be left which, although they will not prevent a dog from winning in the ring, can sadly blemish a beautiful animal.

Another disadvantage to housing your Danes in numbers is that a 'boss dog' is likely to emerge from the pack. This particular dog can literally rule the roost, and cause others in the same kennel to develop a timidity which they would not otherwise show.

When building a kennel it is better to err on the large side rather than the small. Make it at least 6 ft. (or better still 8 ft.) square. The ready-made sheds which can be bought anywhere are excellent. In either case line with hardboard, for this will insulate against extremes of cold or heat, and also prevent chilling. Have a window for light and air, and try to arrange for one run per kennel; in this way your dogs can have their freedom the whole day, and need only be shut away for the night. Cleaning is thus reduced to a minimum, and one can also leave the dogs for some hours knowing they will be safe and sound.

The runs should be large, preferably at least 25 ft. by 15 ft., which not only gives your dogs sufficient room to move around freely but obviates the tendency of Great Danes to damage the ends of their tails. Grass runs are ideal, but we only dream about them; how quickly the lovely grass turns into a mud patch! I do not think concrete runs are perfect, but they seem to be the simplest and cleanest, and cleanliness is essential so far as the dogs are concerned. Have a fairly good slope in order to avoid dampness, and avoid having the surface too smooth or the dogs may slip up. If there are a couple of wooden platforms (about 4 ft. by 3 ft.) in each run, then the dogs can rest on these during the day if they don't wish to go into the kennels; to have them sitting around on cold, wet concrete is asking for trouble. It is amazing how even the youngest of puppies will seize any opportunity to get off the cold ground and on to a platform or box.

Inside your kennel, have a wooden bench, again well off the floor and not a fixture, so that it can be removed for easy cleaning. A wooden board at least 6 in. deep round the bench makes it into a kind of box, and will prevent the bedding from spilling over the edge.

The door of the kennel can be fixed in a partly opened position with a simple rod, so that the dogs can run in and out and yet be protected from the weather. Great Danes do not seem to relish the rain, so on a very wet day you will find that by the time you have cleaned and exercised them they will be happy to return to their snug kennels.

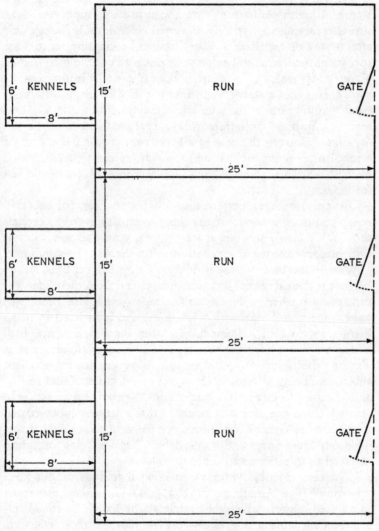

FIG. 15   Plan of kennels

Dogs which are housed in dry, draught-free kennels do not require heat, and will keep in excellent health under these conditions.

When constructing the run, have chain-link fencing at least 5 ft. high, with angle irons or wooden posts as supports. Make sure that this fencing is properly erected, since nothing looks worse after a year or two than a dilapidated and collapsing fence. One successful method is to bridge your posts across the top; that is, if your posts are, say, 6 ft. apart, bolt a 6 ft. piece of iron across the top. This makes a strong rigid frame, and will prevent the dogs from dragging down the wire when they jump up at it. The best way to stop them from burrowing out at the bottom of the run (or digging out in the case of a grass run) is to have a 4 in. or 6 in. plank running right round the bottom and securely stapled to the wire. This really makes a first-class job, which should last for years.

Use only the very best quality felt for roofing, for this will repay you in long service many times over. Creosote the kennels thoroughly inside and out at least once a year, and this will not only preserve them but serve to disinfect them at the same time.

What is the best type of bedding? We have never liked straw, because it can carry fleas, lice and mange, and from these menaces can spring further problems such as tapeworms. Straw seems to have some peculiar attraction for dogs, and is inclined to make them want to foul it immediately, even on a clean straw bed. Wood wool is by far the best type of bedding, but the price is almost prohibitive. Wood shavings, however, are an excellent substitute, being absolutely clean, easy to dispose of and readily and cheaply acquired. It is important to provide a good, substantial, thick bed, for it is essential that a large smooth-coated breed like the Great Dane should not be lying on a hard surface. This can cause sores and corns, which besides being unsightly can lead to infections and other troubles.

How can one discover a water bowl that dogs cannot keep upsetting? The Americans have a good idea: they use small galvanised buckets which they hitch by the handle to the chain-link fencing with a dog clip—very simple and most effective. Alternatively, bowls can be purchased with a hoop attachment

Thomas Fall

Ch. Survey of Leesthorphill

Aus. Ch. Rollo of Warwick

Am. and Can. Ch. Danelagh's Ottar

Am. Ch. Danelagh's Fergus

Ake Wintzell

Int. Ch. Harmony Hill Linda of Airways

BEST OF BREED-VARIETY

Evelyn M. Shafer

The author in America, with Ch. Heathers Hrothgar

C. M. Cooke

Ch. Clausentum Magnus

Anne Cumbers

Ch. Clausentum Gulliver

into which they sit, and this can be bolted on to the fencing at the head level of the dog. Do not forget that your water bowls should always be emptied at night, for rats can be attracted to water, and are also carriers of serious—sometimes fatal—diseases which can affect both humans and animals.

Another effective and cheaper method is to buy suitable bowls, and then make a cement block into which they fit. It is surprisingly easy to find suitable reasonably priced dishes at surplus and army trading stores.

Now to the question of exercising. A Dane, like any other dog, requires sufficient for his needs. For example, the game little terrier, brimming over with energy, can do with as much as or more than any big breed; then there are the small gun dogs, especially bred to do many miles in a day, and they could probably far outstrip a Great Dane. Although the Dane is a large dog he is a placid and easily contented animal who requires no more exercise than can easily be coped with by the average person, whether in town or country, flat or mansion.

The owner is obviously the prevailing influence. I have known of people living in large estates and big houses who have not been nearly so conscientious about exercising and caring for their dogs as another person living in very much more confined and modest conditions. A butler or gardener is often instructed to 'attend to Jason's exercise and feeding', but the dog does not receive the same care and attention as his brother living in what would appear to be humbler circumstances.

An adult Great Dane requires no more exercise than the normal pet dog: a morning walk with a romp in a nearby park or recreation ground, the run of the garden as he wants during the day, and another walk in the evening. Of course you could train your Dane to do twenty miles behind a horse each day if you so wished, but then you could also do the same with a beagle or poodle! The main thing is to keep the balance the same—don't take your dog on a twenty-mile trek on one day and on a twenty-minute walk the next.

The feeding of the adult dog is important, whether he is being kept for show purposes or as a pet. See that he has one main meal per day, perhaps a small breakfast, but his large and important meal later on. Where possible raw fresh meat should be given. Tinned meats are very good, but we would recommend you to ring the changes to avoid monotony. After all, we ourselves might be very fond of tinned salmon, but if we ate it every day we should probably not keep in the best of health, besides being bored to tears with the same dish. Bullock's tripes are still reasonably priced, and can be fed raw if they are fresh and have been thoroughly washed. A friendly butcher will often help with leftover scraps which can be bought quite cheaply, and for one-dog owners there are likely to be certain leftovers from the household table which will always be appreciated.

Always feed a good quality dog biscuit; an occasional raw egg and perhaps a pint of milk do not come amiss. Remember too that you are feeding not only your companion dog, but an animal which will protect you more than any insurance policy against burglars, so do not begrudge him a treat from time to time.

There is no short cut to producing good dogs. Trying to economise on good food proves to be false economy in the end. A common saying of some of the early breeders was 'half the pedigree goes in at the mouth', and this still holds true today.

General care of your dog or dogs should always be foremost in your mind, and the kennel owner who has kept his numbers to the minimum will find he has ample time for all the little extras such as grooming, cleaning of the ears, and regular de-fleaing. The best-cared-for dogs can catch fleas and lice when out on their daily exercising, and a regular powdering with one of the recommended brands keeps these pests at bay.

In the interests of your young stock, it is best to house them in a completely different section from your adult dogs, and to keep them completely isolated. The main reason for this is to reduce infection to a minimum; many show dogs have brought distemper and hardpad home to their kennels, and promising puppies have been wiped out. Even if you have already safe-guarded your older dogs with their various inoculations, they—like human beings—can act as carriers of disease, and this is where the real danger lies. The unsuspecting breeder can all too quickly find he has sick and dying puppies around him, and will wonder how the infection ever reached his well-run establishment.

Another advantage of having a puppy section away from the main kennels is that you can sell your puppies with confidence, knowing that they have not been subjected to the risk of any virus infection.

It is also relevant to mention here that when potential buyers visit your establishment to view puppies, you should check that they have not been visiting other kennels, for they too can be carriers of infection. It is surprising how some families decide to go on a tour of kennels on Saturdays and Sundays; they can quite innocently leave in their wake a trail of trouble, expense and heartbreak.

To sum up: kennel and bed your dogs in clean, dry, draughtfree conditions; see that they have plenty of fresh air and light; feed them a well-balanced, sensible diet; exercise daily according to their needs, and ensure that they are regularly groomed.

9

Showing

So you want to show your dog? A good idea, and why not? The great beauty of the 'dog game' is that the field is always wide open to the newcomer with a good animal.

You will find that the same people often win at shows; this does not mean that the judges are dishonest, but merely that the well-known and established breeders are more likely to show the best dogs. After all, they have achieved their fame through consistently breeding and showing good stock, and over a period of time—perhaps many years—have built up a reputation for having some of the top Great Danes.

Pay no attention, therefore, to the Jonahs who will all too readily tell you that you will never win because you are not known. This is ridiculous since nobody starts by being famous in any field. Always remember that the top people of today were the unknowns of yesterday, and that tomorrow's successes will come from the beginners of today.

There are a number of things you must do, before even entering for a show. Firstly, join one of the breed clubs; this will bring you into contact with all the current developments in the breed. Most of the clubs run several breed shows each year, and these will give you an opportunity to meet other breeders and fanciers. Also, a number of the clubs produce either a monthly or a quarterly magazine which members find helpful, and which can be a mine of information to the novice.

The policy of a breed club is to further the interests of the Great Dane at all times, while also safeguarding the breed and its welfare generally. Naturally, such a club has certain limitations, but its prime objective should be to help and instruct the novice owner, at the same time fostering suitable people who will later become judges themselves. Breed clubs are always on the look out for potential judges, but the operative word is 'suitable'. One expects experience, integrity, competence and temperament from the ideal judge, but it is perhaps more difficult than one would imagine to find all these qualities combined in one person.

Membership of a breed club, therefore, is in your present and future interest.

Buy one of the weekly dog papers such as *Our Dogs* or *Dog World*, which will give you full details of all forthcoming shows throughout the country, critiques of past prizewinners and interesting news written by leading authorities on Great Danes. In the show advertisements you will also find the various classifications listed, together with the respective judges, and a list of names and addresses of show secretaries from whom entry forms and schedules can be obtained.

You will find your breed column of the greatest interest: the writers are always delighted to hear from people who are keen on the breed and will be prepared to take up various points and have them discussed. This column also serves as a mouthpiece, and it is up to you to take advantage of the opportunity to put forward for discussion any problems and ideas which may come to your mind. Weekly breed writers are always looking for news, and if constructive criticisms can sometimes be added, this makes for interest and generally stimulates feelings within the breed.

I suggest you also visit a few dog shows to get some idea of what really goes on. You will have the opportunity to discuss your breed with other Dane exhibitors, and if time permits the judge will also be happy to give you a few words of advice.

Study the various winners, and see how your own dog compares with them. Remember too that a dog or bitch winning a first prize is only as good as the competition on that day; in other words, an animal may win two or three firsts on one day in a mediocre competition, but several days later the same dog may be lucky to achieve fourth place at another show. The fourth place at the second show may in fact be a better win than the higher awards on the earlier occasion, for the competition may have been of a very much higher standard. Then again, different judges see different dogs in a different light. A good judge always assesses the dogs as a 'whole', but all dogs have faults and it is the varying emphasis put on each animal's faults or virtues that accounts for the fluctuations in placings from show to show.

Another point to be borne in mind is that your dog can look marvellous one week, yet be very much out of form the next. So many exhibitors make the mistake of hawking their young stock from show to show, and consequently run the risk of their becoming 'show-tired'. The average puppy needs plenty of time at home to sleep and grow, and should not be campaigned round the shows; an occasional outing at a show is fine for the promising youngster, who will enjoy the occasion as much as his owner, but he still has all his life in front of him to really make a name as a show dog. He will soon become bored with the proceedings if he is carted up and down the countryside two or three times a week while still so young.

You will soon find that the judges fall into two categories: the specialist and the all-rounder. I feel that the specialist judge is wrongly named, and it would be better to refer to him quite simply as a 'breed judge'. A Great Dane judge will be someone who has bred and shown Great Danes with some success for several years; someone of this description will have acquired a detailed knowledge of the breed by virtue of the fact that he (or she) has bred puppies, dealt with Great Danes from day to day, and attended and shown at many shows where the breed has been classified. On the other hand, the all-rounder judge is some-one who has made a lifelong study of dogs in general, and has usually bred and owned a number of good animals in several breeds.

It follows, therefore, that an all-breed judge may be judging Great Danes without having owned or bred that particular breed; but this is nothing for you as an owner to worry about since you will probably be showing under a man or woman who is so steeped in knowledge of all that is required in a good dog, that he or she has forgotten more than many others will ever know. Correct balance, soundness, make and shape come easily to their eye, for without these attributes no dog can be truly great in any breed.

Both the breed judges and the all-rounders have important roles to play. The breed judge constantly brings us back to type, and the essential characteristics of the Great Dane, and he knows also the finer points and details of the breed. My own personal feeling, however, is that many specialists cannot 'see the wood for the trees' and will often put a dog to win which excels in certain points but is not a good specimen when taken as a whole. An all-breed judge does tend to have a wider vision, and judges his dogs on a broader aspect for construction, soundness, ring presence, style and personality, all of which are important when he is considering his award.

There is no doubt that a breed is at its best when it is judged regularly by both specialists and all-rounders, for between them they keep an essential balance which can easily be lost if both are not allowed to contribute their wisdom and knowledge. There is a tendency for the specialists (for want of a better name) to become unduly restricted in their approach, and as one famous breeder commented to me, 'all-rounders bring sanity back to a breed'.

Now to consider the types of show for which you may enter your dog. The smallest is the four-class Exemption Show, generally held on a Saturday afternoon or on summer evenings, and run for charity. A well-known local personality in the dog world usually adjudicates, and it is amazing the number of entries this type of show attracts. I have seen classes of eighty and ninety, but no one takes this kind of show too seriously, and they are considered by most people to be just good fun. They also provide an opportunity for you to obtain some practice with your Great Dane in readiness for a larger show.

The next up the scale is the Sanction Show, usually made up to twenty to twenty-five classes and normally consisting of Variety Classes. Famous judges quite often officiate at events of this kind, and here you may well obtain a first-class opinion on your Great Dane.

Then there are Members' Limited Shows, which can be quite large events and may be confined to either breed or variety. As in the case of Sanction Shows, champions and Challenge Certificate winners are barred from competition, but you are still likely to be competing against some high-class dogs.

The Open Show is one of the most important. Champions are allowed to compete at these events, and there are invariably generous classifications for many breeds, with breed judges for their respective types. First prizes at Open Shows are also important to young dogs or bitches under the age of eighteen months, for a winner in a breed class at an Open Show counts one point towards the Kennel Club Junior Warrant.

Last but not least there are the Championship Shows, the classic events of the year. There are three annually which cater for Great Danes only, and a further two dozen are held throughout the year at different locations all over the British Isles, culminating in Cruft's which is internationally recognised as the most important show in 'dogdom'.

Championship Shows are the only opportunity for the breeders to make their dogs or bitches into champions, and this is no easy feat. A dog or bitch must win three Challenge Certificates under three different judges before the coveted title of *Champion* can be added to its name, and bearing in mind that there is only one Challenge Certificate for the dog and bitch at each Championship Show, the difficulty of gaining this award will be appreciated. Dogs which are already champions can still be shown, and frequently win many more certificates, making it harder still for the good new animals to break through.

Although our system of making champions is difficult, I also think it is excellent. Cheap champions are rare, and whilst this is so, British champions will continue to be among the best in the world.

First prizes at Championship Shows also count towards the Junior Warrant, and a Red Card won at these classic events carries three points. For a dog to win the Junior Warrant he must gain twenty-five points before he is eighteen months of age. Kennel Club Junior Warrants are not automatically awarded, and the claim must be made by the owner to the Kennel Club itself.

Having carefully considered the various types of show, you can now make your choice as to where you first want to exhibit your dog. Do not forget to check that all his papers are in order, i.e. that he is correctly registered at the Kennel Club by the breeder and that you have duly completed the necessary form for his transfer from the breeder to yourself. Should there be any doubt, write to the Registration Department, the Kennel Club, 1 Clarges Street, London W1Y 8AB, giving full details to avoid any unnecessary delay.

A breeder now has to register the litter as a litter pack. To be done in three weeks of birth, this will cost £1. The second stage is the individual registering of each puppy by the breeder, or the new owner. It will cost the breeder £1 per puppy and a non-breeder, £1·50. This now places the new puppy in the 'basic register'. A transfer to the new owner will cost a further £2. For an animal to be shown or bred from, it must then be registered into the 'active' list of the K.C. This means another fee of £1·50.

Another preliminary before showing your puppy can be to join a local obedience class, as mentioned in Chapter 5. It is well worth while for any Dane owner—whether interested in showing or not—to attend these clasess for a short period. Here you will be advised on how to school your dog firmly and kindly, so that you eventually have a well-mannered dog which is a pleasure and joy to own. Many obedience classes also provide weekly ringcraft instruction. For the newcomer it is most helpful to receive tips on how best to show your dog and stress his good points.

From the time your dog is a tiny puppy, try to make him stand still for a short time every day. Speak quietly to him all the while; the tone of your voice alone will be sufficient for him to know whether you are pleased with him or not. Look at his teeth, feel his limbs and generally accustom him to being handled. Also teach him to walk on a loose lead in a straight line, as this will be important when the judge wants to assess his movements.

There is no sight more disappointing than an unschooled Great Dane in the ring. So often the fault does not lie with the dog or the handler, but is brought about by the owner's ignorance. The dog can appear to be shy or even bad tempered when in fact he is neither, but just lacking the esential discipline he should have had as a growing puppy.

The day of your first show dawns at last. By now your dog should be at the peak of condition, with a gleaming coat from regular grooming and firm, strong muscles. He should be carrying just the right amount of weight, not so much as to spoil his out-line and not so little that people make unkind remarks about your 'greyhound'. Pack a show bag for your charge, since you will require his grooming kit, a bowl for water, a blanket for his bench, a strong collar and benching chain. His show lead should be made of good leather, half an inch wide with a ring on the end; this is what is known as a slip lead, is ideal in the ring, and can be obtained from most good dog shops or dog stands at the show, or made by a saddler.

Do not take food for him unless you are to be away for many hours. A fit dog will not come to any harm through missing a meal. Even the most placid animal can be affected by being out of his usual environment, and prefers to return home before eating. At all the big shows excellent biscuits and meat can be bought on the day if wished, and I think this is far simpler than carrying unnecessary excess luggage around.

The Schedule will tell you the time the judging commences, and a few days before the show you will receive an Exhibitor's Pass through the post. Allow yourself sufficient time to get to the show; make sure that there is no rush and tear, and that both you and your dog are benched ready and waiting for the judging at least half an hour before this is due to begin. When you arrive an attendant will direct you to the benches for Great Danes; the benching runs in numerical order, and you will have on either side other exhibitors whose names begin with the same letter of the alphabet.

Your dog will probably take to his bench fairly quickly, but if he is a little overawed by the proceedings do not worry him. Give him time to settle, and gently persuade him to sit down. Make sure that he has a strong leather collar, attach one end of the benching chain securely to this and the other to the special ring attachment on the bench itself. Check that the chain is of sufficient length to allow the dog to move freely on his bench, but not long enough to enable him to jump off. You will have the opportunity to exercise him for fifteen minutes at a time, but at all other times (except when he is being judged in the ring) he should be benched according to Kennel Club rules.

If you become really interested in showing, join your local canine club. Here you can meet local breeders, some of whom may be famous in their respective categories, and will find that you can learn much from them which will help you in your new-found interest. As time goes by, take part in the club activities, and if the opportunity arises become a member of the committee; in this way you will also be able to further the interests of the Great Dane. Many clubs now organise lectures, teach-ins, film shows, and so on, in addition to matches and rallies which—besides being enjoyable social events—are also good show and ring experiences for your dog.

Do not let yourself become so obsessed with the importance of winning that you put yourself in danger of having either a nervous breakdown or a stomach ulcer! I am quite sure there are some people who do not have the right temperament for exhibiting dogs. After all, failure to win at a dog show is hardly the end of the world, and unless you can take the rough patches with the smooth it is best not to even consider embarking on such a hobby as showing dogs.

Remember also that your dog is only as good as his condition on the day that you are actually showing him. Varying competition plus changing conditions can so often account for a dog being up at a show one day and down the next.

There are two golden rules: firstly, never show your dog unless he is in tip-top condition and well schooled. If you know you have a good animal, go into the ring and show him with confidence—dogs are highly sensitive to atmosphere and moods, and will reflect your confidence in their own behaviour. Secondly, make up your mind to enjoy dog showing. Far too many people take the whole thing much too seriously; after all, there is always another day, and the old saying that 'every dog has his day' still has a ring of truth about it.

Great Danes at Home and Abroad

IN this chapter we shall be dealing with the more recent history of the breed, though for obvious reasons I shall not be mentioning prominent breeders and exhibitors who are active in Great Danes at the present time.

At the end of hostilities in 1945 breeders in the United Kingdom were faced with making a fresh start. Many of them who had been well known at the outbreak of war, when they were forced to give up their dogs, did not seem to have the enthusiasm and interest to return to the 'dog-game' and play an active part.

Mr. J. V. Rank had been able to keep together a very small nucleus of his already famous and established Ouborough strain, and Miss Muriel Osborn of Blendon fame had also kept her strain alive by a limited amount of breeding. Another kennel which figured in the immediate post-war build-up was that of Mrs. Rowberry, whose Winome Great Danes figure in many of today's pedigrees. She produced several champions, the most famous probably being Ch. Juan of Winome which became the first post-war champion in the breed.

Mrs. G. M. Clayton, who kept a small, quality kennel in Lincolnshire, produced a first-class litter by Rebellion of Ouborough (who was bred in wartime), and from this came the lovely fawn bitch Ch. Bon Adventure of Barvae which also had the honour to be the first bitch in the breed to gain her title after the war.

During the war years only one kennel in the country continued to breed on a large scale; this was the Ladymead, whose Great Danes were owned by Mrs. G. M. Jewell of Bristol. Although no Ladymead dogs or bitches ever became champions in England,

Mrs. Jewell bred and sold many puppies which were later bred from, and therefore had quite a far-reaching influence on the breed. Her most famous dog was a huge golden fawn called Hyperion of Ladymead; he was extensively used for breeding, and his reputation was built up mainly on his great height and his appearance in the famous film *The Wicked Lady*. He was never exhibited for competition, which seemed a pity, for he would still have been in his prime when the first post-war shows took place. In fact, his only appearance was at a dog show in Bristol when he was entered 'Not for Competition': here all the V.I.P. and special publicity treatment was laid on, the huge fawn dog spending most of the day reclining on a couch being guarded by two uniformed attendants specially hired for the occasion!

In harlequins Mrs. G. Hatfield of Sudbury fame was still alive, although she now felt she was past returning to the show ring for she was the senior Great Dane breeder and had been exhibiting since 1906. We were among the last to have a litter from one of her stud dogs when we bred a litter of harlequins to Zaynos of Sudbury.

Miss M. Lomas was upholding the reputation of the harlequins at this time with her dogs which she exhibited very successfully under the name 'Wideskies'. These carried all the best bloodlines, also going back to the Sudbury strain. They became very famous after the war, and several good animals appeared in the show ring, the best of them perhaps being Ch. Frost of the Wideskies.

These were the principal names which played a leading part in re-establishing the Great Dane in Britain after the war. One of the most important bitches was the lovely brindle Ch. Ryot of Ouborough, bred by Mr. J. V. Rank and later owned by Mrs. Connie Robb of Foxbar fame who lived in Scotland. The golden fawn Ch. Royalism of Ouborough—one of the best movers in the breed—also had a brilliant show career, winning numerous Challenge Certificates and siring no less than ten champions, still a post-war record for the breed in the United Kingdom.

Ch. Royalism mated to Ch. Ryot produced an exceptional litter, in that the three sisters—Ch. Raet of Ouborough, Ch. Rindle of Ouborough and Ch. Riotus of Foxbar—all gained their titles in the show ring. Ch. Raet was a beautifully made and sound-moving brindle bitch which belonged to Mr. Rank, and had an excellent show career including a win of the Non-Sporting Group at Cruft's in 1950.

In the meantime Mr. Rank had acquired a fine upstanding fawn dog from Germany, Hector of Ouborough. He had an interesting story, for as the mascot of the 51st Highland Regiment he had served in Italy, Greece and France, and when the regiment was disbanded he was presented to Mr. Rank. Although he was obviously descended from some of the illustrious pre-war German dogs, he had no papers and for this reason was recorded 'pedigree unknown'. He was mated to a bitch called Relique of Ouborough, and this mating produced a dog named Kalandus of Ouborough. The mating of Kalandus to Ch. Raet (a daughter of Ch. Royalism) produced what was to become the greatest winner in the history of the breed—Ch. Elch Edler of Ouborough.

Elch Edler, a fine large dog, was to bring the Ouborough kennels—already holders of most records for the breed—to the peak of success, for in 1953 he won Supreme Champion when he went Best in Show All Breeds at Cruft's, the largest dog show in the world. Sadly, Mr. Rank had died in 1951, when Ch. Elch Edler was just a puppy, but his manager for all those years, Mr. W. G. Siggers, had the outstanding achievement of piloting this dog through to the greatest win which can be accorded to any dog and its handler.

Shown as a puppy, Elch Edler gained his title in three straight shows and was a full champion at twelve months of age. He was never extensively campaigned, but had a brilliant show record. Although this dog has ultimately had a greater impact on the breed than any other since the war, as so often happens he was not appreciated to the fullest extent by the breeders of his day. Those who did use him had excellent results: he produced several champions, and it is through his sons and daughters that his influence can be seen in all fawn and brindle pedigrees today.

Miss Osborn bred many good post-war champions, the most important perhaps being Ch. Bonhommie of Blendon, a big brindle dog who was a contemporary of Ch. Elch Edler of Ouborough, and also amassed many Challenge Certificates. It has been mainly on the Ouborough, Blendon and Winome blood-lines that the foundations of the present-day Great Danes have been built. Today there are many breeders who developed their strain and type on the basis of 'choice and selection' from breeding stock available from these three strains, which were particularly dominant in the decade immediately following the Second World War.

The late Mrs. Marjorie Green bred several good champions under the name of Arranton. Mr. and Mrs. S. Laming had a short but successful career in the breed; after mating their bitch Radiance of Ladymead to Ch. Royalism of Ouborough she bred a very famous litter which contained Ch. Dawnlight of Ickford and International Champions Anndale Moonlight of Ickford and Anndale Royalight of Ickford. The last two were purchased and campaigned in the show ring by Mr. J. McKee of Belfast.

Since that time the breed has become more and more popular, and the current registrations of puppies recorded at the Kennel Club are higher than ever before. I wish I could say that the quality of the Great Dane has improved too, but unfortunately this is not the case, and the last decade has seen a lowering in the general overall standard of excellence. This has largely been brought about by breeding on an extensive scale, which has unfortunately not always been in the best interests of the breed.

Judges are frequently saddened by the standard of exhibits before them at shows; this is not to say that there are no good specimens to be found, but they are very much in the minority at the present time. The fault does not in the main lie with estab-lished breeders, but more often with the one-Dane owner who breeds from an inferior specimen and often uses an equally unsuitable dog as a mate.

On the other hand, breeders owning good stud dogs can help to improve the position enormously by encouraging new-comers to breed only from good bitches, and also by being highly selective in the bitches which they allow to be mated to their own dogs. After all, dogs are placed at stud 'to approved bitches only'! But how often does an owner of a stud dog refuse a bitch? This policy, if adopted, would rapidly pay dividends in a complete upgrading of the overall standard. We should all concern ourselves with the fact that eminent overseas breeders who visit leading shows in the U.K. are not impressed with the general standard of our breed as it is today.

So far as developments in America are concerned, I have on several occasions had the honour to judge the breed there, and am able to speak from first-hand knowledge. I was fortunate that on these occasions I had good representative entries, and in addition I attended the great Westminster Show and the Chicago International Show, considered to be the two most important dog shows in the United States. This experience has enabled me to see many American Great Danes, coming from a very wide area.

At the present time the Americans are far ahead of their counterparts here in the United Kingdom. Of course, they have some mediocre animals, but these are not so commonly seen as in England, and the American Danes do not suffer from the constructional faults often shown by our Danes nowadays. Bad mouths, straight shoulders, steep croups—all of these are faults which worry many of our serious breeders but are seldom seen in America.

One may well enquire how this happy state of affairs has come about in America. The main reason appears to be that, like us, they had very many superb German imports brought into the country prior to the war. These were used to build up the breed to a high standard, as was happening at the same time in England, but the Second World War did not have the devastating effect in the States that it had on Britain and most of the Continent. It is important to remember that American breeders, although affected to some degree, were not restricted to the same extent as we were.

At the outbreak of the last war literally thousands and thousands of dogs in various breeds were destroyed; consequently years— and sometimes a lifetime—of valuable work building up a strain, were in many cases completely lost overnight. Prior to the war the Americans had already produced many fine Great Danes, as indeed we had in England, but they were in a much happier position in that they were able to retain their stock and continue to improve their standards until they reached the overall high quality which exists today.

The top American Great Danes have to be seen to be fully appreciated. American breeders have succeeded in producing well-balanced, immensely powerful animals, which at the same time have the beautiful refinement and elegance which is the hallmark of a good specimen. Their big, deep, strong bodies are superb, and their quarters are strong, broad and well let down. Light eyes and faulty mouths are taboo. In my opinion American breeders are to be congratulated on the fine animals they are producing at the present time, many of which frequently take important wins of groups and Best in Show at the major shows in the States.

Some of the important Danes of the immediate post-war era were Ch. Ajax Telemon, a great sire, Ch. Fergus of Daynemouth, Ch. Niel of Brae Tarn and Ch. Jansen of Brae Tarn. The greatest sire of all time, however, was Ch. Vakecks Gallant Cavalier, who sired twenty-two champions and was a grandson of Ch. Wasden v. Loland of Vakeck. Ch. Wasden had previously held the record by having sired thirteen champions, and he too was directly descended from the immortal Dolf v.d. Saalburg who had been described in his day as 'the greatest sire in the world'.

In 1946 forty-four dogs gained their title, and in 1947 forty-five finished, including the great Ch. Senta, who, besides being one of the most famous show bitches, also proved a particularly good brood bitch and was thought by many to be the best bitch of the decade. Mr. William Gilbert, one of the senior breeders, has had many notable Danes through the years, and many of his famous 'Gilberts' are to be found in pedigrees today. Another famous dog who completed his title in 1947 was Ch. Fury, who also had an outstanding ring career. Ch. Freddons Noble Lady was a superb harlequin, and Ch. Gilbert Dolf Crusader and Ch. Gilbert Glory Adele are others who have left their mark on the breed.

Ch. Dane Edens Samson was another famous animal of that period, as were the beautiful Ch. Brenda of Brae Tarn, Ch. Heide of Brae Tarn who produced fifteen champions, Ch. Sieglinda of Riverside, Ch. Duchess of Zel-Thor, Ch. Creightons Sweet Sue and Ch. Winged Victory. Other top winners were Ch. Amber of Thimble Farm, Ch. Gleann Planetree Gal and Ch. Bornholms Cassanova.

The Daynemouths are another line which has played a leading role in the breed, and appear in the pedigrees of many of the present-day winners. Founded in the early 1940s, Daynemouth combined Send and Brae Tarn blood-lines to establish this most successful kennel and produce many champions. Until the 1950s, the outstanding kennels which were taking the plum prizes and consistently winning high awards were Brae Tarn, Carliss, Duysters, Ehmling, Roxdane and Gilbert.

As with this country, I am not mentioning the famous American breeders who are actively involved with showing and breeding Great Danes at present, other than Mr. and Mrs. Gerrard Johnston with their Marydane dogs, and Mrs. Rosemarie Roberts with her Dinro strain. These breeders, together with Bill Gilbert, are amongst America's most senior enthusiasts and are household names wherever Great Danes are discussed. Through their long connections with the breed they have created strains which are dominant.

A prominent dog of the war years was Ch. The Duke of Roxdane, who won Best of Breed at Westminster in 1940. He was a magnificent animal, sire of excellent puppies, and his owner received a standing offer of $5,000 for him; however, like so many dogs, this one was priceless to his owner!

Famous dogs are often surrounded by amusing stories or tales of chance, and it seems that luck played a large part for Mr. Ehmling and The Duke. Mr. Jacob Steinbacher telephoned to ask Mr. Ehmling if he had a really good four-month-old puppy for sale, as he himself was unable to help a client who wished to be suited immediately. If Mr. Ehmling could produce a puppy at once, he could in return take his pick from the Steinbacher stud litter resulting from a mating of Ch. Steinbacher King and Rino von Bremen.

Mr. Ehmling did happen to have a most promising four-month-old Dane which he was keeping for himself, but Mr. Steinbacher was a very good friend whom he was happy to oblige. He gambled and he won, for the stud puppy he subsequently chose became Ch. The Duke of Roxdane.

Bill Gilbert (now affectionately called 'Pop' Gilbert), who in his time was the top eastern breeder of fawns and brindles, came into the breed by sheer chance. Needing a large watch dog, he bought one for $5 without realising at the time that the animal was a Great Dane. Both he and Mrs. Gilbert fell in love with 'Pat', and decided to go to the dogs entirely! They achieved spectacular results, and Ch. Senta which they bred is considered one of the best Great Dane bitches ever.

For those who never saw Ch. Senta, Bertha Souberyrand Gautheir gives us a glimpse back in time to one of the all-time greats of the breed:

'Senta has a superbly feminine head, more mask desirable, yes. But with her tremendous size, a mask of depth might make her look masculine. Senta has a magnificent front, spring of rib, deep brisket, denoting plenty of heart and lung room—all that could be desired in body. The croup and tail set is excellent, and hindquarters absolutely correct. From within, there is a style and flash seldom seen in the show ring, regardless of breed.

From the betterment of the breed angle, the owner of Senta, Mrs. Walter Schroeder, bred her Champion twice, to Champion Gilberts Dolf Crusader. From the first litter came Champion Senta's Astrid—also a constant Best of Breed winner. Astrid is very like her dam, but lacks the Senta showmanship. To see this pair in the ring, the dam and her get, is a sight the discerning Great Dane lover will never forget.'

In America professional handling plays a large part in the dog show game, but this does not mean that a one-dog owner who handles his own dog cannot win. Being such a vast country, America particularly lends itself to professional handling, for many owners would not have the time to be away from home showing their animals. Shows are often held in circuits, which means that one may be away for a week or so, showing day after day—hard on the dogs and hard on the exhibitors! Apart from the time factor, it is often cheaper for owners to hire a handler than endeavour to cover all the shows themselves.

Some people in England seem to have the idea that professional handling is not in the best interests of dogdom, but I cannot follow this line of thinking at all. These professionals have to be good in order to win, for they are competing against others of similar skill and experience who only take on the handling of the best dogs which are offered to them.

Living on a small island as we do here, showing is a comparatively easy job, and we are able to exhibit dogs in Scotland one day and be back home in the south of England the next. Therefore there is not the same need for professional handlers in the British Isles, but I would not in any case agree that they 'spoil a breed', for the final result rests with the judge, and if he is good he will make the right decisions.

One of the impressions of America which remains with me is of a class of Danes being handled by professionals, each showing his or her charge to perfection and getting the very last ounce from the dog or bitch concerned.

So far as the wider aspects of the Continent are concerned, friends in those countries have been kind enough to obtain information for me. In Belgium, for example, there is a famous kennel breeding all colours which houses eighty to a hundred adults. There is also a wide choice of shows there, and exhibitors frequently enter their dog for these events in Belgium, France, Switzerland, Germany, Italy and Holland.

In an article by Mme Desenfans, of Belgium, who travels thousands of miles annually as an exhibitor, she says: 'I have been struck by the general fact that German Danes are rarely well shown, there appears to be a lack of show training for both dog and owner, accompanied by a nervousness of the exhibitor.' She further adds 'that German Danes, on occasions, lack the substance that the breed should have'. These remarks coming from a leading expert are most interesting, for they give the impression that the *Deutsche Doggen* of the present are not up to the high standard of their pre-war ancestors. It is important to remember, however, that the Second World War must have brought their breeding programmes to a halt, and the general effect on the progress of the breed was probably even more devastating than that experienced by British breeders at the same time.

Photographs and information brought home by some of our leading all-round judges show that some very fine specimens of

Great Dane are to be found in Sweden, brought about by clever blending of American and German blood-lines. Today they have several very fine Great Danes which are able to win Best in Show awards at the premier continental events.

Switzerland remains strong in blues, blacks and harlequins, and some good harlequin stock was imported from there a few years ago by Mr. Martin Summers. The main names behind Swiss Great Danes are Dr. Vollenweider, who was particularly prominent in the late 1920s and early 1930s; Mrs. Richard-Keller, owner of some of the best brindles and fawns for many years; and Mr. and Mrs. Mohler for harlequins. Other famous Swiss breeders were Walter Meyer, Zwinger von Rutterkhoen, Josef Bislin, Zwinger von Eichenberg and Dr. Bornhauser. None of them, however, was particularly interested in the blue variety, and it was Madame Magda Bergen who forty-five years ago became interested in this colour and specialised in blues. Her dogs, bred under the name of 'Sans Soucis', are known the world over.

Great Danes in Australia remain rare, but there has always been a small nucleus of interest. An import which had great influence was the honey fawn bitch Riotus of Foxbar, by Ch. Royalism of Ouborough ex. Ch. Ryot. She was sent out by Mrs. Connie Robb to Mr. W. Spilstead, and had an extremely good show career, winning all the principal shows, including Best in Show at Melbourne Royal. The late Mrs. Joan Drinkwater, who kept a very small and select kennel in England, sent two very good brindle specimens to Australia—Ch. Diamond of Ashthorpe and Ch. Gold of Ashthorpe—who both did very well for the breed in that country.

Great Danes can be found all over the world, but—as has always been the case—it is on the Continent and in America and the United Kingdom that we find the breed numerically very strong. Here there is keen interest which is kept alive by a hard core of enthusiasts, and it is in these countries that the real strength of the Great Dane as a breed still lies.

11

Common Ailments

PROVIDED they are bred from stock which has a healthy, disease-free background, and are themselves correctly housed and reared, Great Danes should remain in generally good health. Good housing conditions, a well-balanced sensible diet, plus the right amount of exercise and grooming, should keep any dog in the pink of condition. It is far wiser to spend money on keeping your dog well in the first place, for when it comes to good feeding and correct housing there is no compromise. Apart from inoculations and whelping, your visits to the veterinary surgeon should be few and far between.

Great Danes, if bred from sturdy strains, are particularly hardy and suffer few ills. However, it is most important to make the right start, with a puppy which has been correctly reared and is strong and healthy in every way. A sickly, miserable puppy is never a good investment, and will be the cause of many heartaches and added expense.

We must accept, however, that dogs—like human beings—may develop some sickness, and then the only thing is to seek expert advice from your vet. An experienced dog breeder will immediately spot a dog which is off colour, whereas the average pet dog owner might not be so quick to assess this, and so often this is the margin which determines whether cure is possible.

Distemper and hardpad (or, as some vets prefer to call it, para-distemper) are still the most feared diseases, for when encountered they bring sadness to those who have to nurse their dogs. Also, it often happens that dogs which recover may be impaired in some way, and quite frequently a weakness is left which remains with them all their lives.

Both these diseases are caused by a virus, which cannot be developed within an animal but must be caught in the first place. Just as we catch influenza and colds, so dogs can catch virus infections from each other. Infected dogs can act as carriers, and for this reason it is always important to keep young puppies completely isolated until they are fully immunised.

Hardpad and distemper are generally found in puppies or young adults, although the older dog is also susceptible if he has not been inoculated. Very early signs are listlessness, usually accompanied by loss of appetite and possibly loose motions. Every hour counts, for the sooner treatment is begun the greater are the chances of effecting a cure. This is where the experienced breeder often scores, for he will call his veterinary surgeon to examine the sick animal immediately. The inexperienced owner so often waits until the next day, by which time the poor dog has rapidly become worse, and the chances of a complete recovery are substantially reduced.

As the disease progresses there is a discharge from the eyes and an occasional cough, and the dog will probably develop chronic diarrhoea. The great secret when treating a dog with a virus infection is to have absolute peace and quiet: he must be comfortably housed, and kept as quiet as possible for a period of several weeks. Sometimes a dog which has suffered a bad attack may appear to have made a complete recovery after a week or so, but this is only the preliminary stage. Many owners are completely foxed over this, and thinking that their dog is now fit, soon allow him to return to a normal life and regular exercise, only to find that subsequent weeks bring fits, hysteria, chorea (St. Vitus's Dance) and paralysis which invariably leads to death.

When one first suspects that a puppy is sick, he should be completely isolated from all other dogs, and in the case of kennels one person should be detailed to look after him exclusively; it is also vital that all clothes and shoes be disinfected before he or she returns to any other dogs. Scrupulous attention must be paid to cleanliness while the risk of infection remains, and all feeding utensils kept entirely separate.

When the vet arrives he may allay your fears, but he is sure to recommend that you should use the utmost care for a few days.

However, if he confirms that the puppy has a virus infection, do not completely despair, for with patience and care you and your dogs can weather the storm.

Naturally prevention is better than cure, and the age in which we live has made the wonder of modern drugs available to us all. Preventions and cures which were unknown to the older breeders only a few years ago are now commonplace. Many of the original breed enthusiasts lived constantly in the shadow of the killer distemper, and one famous pre-war breeder once said, 'I lost more good dogs than I ever showed', which gives an idea of the magnitude of the problem they had to face. When one is keeping a kennel of dogs, it is important to arrange that puppies and young stock are kennelled separately from the show animals. Dogs returning from shows, although themselves protected through inoculations, can all too easily act as a source of infection which they transmit to others.

Another worry which haunts breeders of the giant dogs is a condition known as 'bloat' or 'flatulence'. There are many theories on this, but few seem to give a lead as to what the cause may be. The condition can affect any dog: he will normally appear fit in every way, then quite suddenly he becomes miserable and shows great discomfort, being unable to sit or lie still and generally restless. It then appears obvious that the stomach is rapidly becoming hard and swollen, and tight as a drum (often referred to as 'drum belly'). This is so serious that the only chance of saving the dog's life is to rush him to the nearest vet at once. Delay means almost certain death, for the stomach continues to expand owing to the gases trapped inside, and will eventually rupture, when death will be inevitable. Where the condition is dealt with in time, however, an emergency operation will probably save the dog's life, although a tendency remains for the animal to suffer subsequent attacks.

Bloat and its possible causes remain very much a mystery, but I feel that the basic cause is closely linked with feeding because the condition frequently occurs shortly after a meal. At one time the theory was widely held that it was risky to feed unsoaked dog biscuit, the danger being that this would later swell inside the stomach. This theory is dispelled by modern feeding techniques, however, for the fashion today is to feed mainly 'dry', and the army and police dogs thrive on their diet of dried kibbled biscuit and meat.

I know that many people still soak their dog biscuit in stock overnight, and cannot help wondering if this may be a contributory cause. Having spoken to many experienced people on both sides of the Atlantic about bloat, I found that a common fear was thundery weather, for it seems that when the atmosphere is sultry there is more chance of having a dog succumb to this illness. It is well known that thundery conditions can easily sour meat stock, and food fed to a dog in this condition could so easily cause a stomach upset leading to bloat.

In case I should alarm anyone, I would add that during twenty-five years of keeping Great Danes we have only experienced two cases of this illness in our own kennel: a small percentage considering there are usually at least two dozen adults in the kennel at a time. Clever professional veterinary brains have from time to time sought to find the cause, but no extensive and detailed research has yet been undertaken. For although bloat remains a curse, it has not been felt that the proportion of deaths is sufficiently high to warrant the vast expenditure which would be required to conduct an experiment of this kind. In the meantime, my advice to owners is to watch carefully how you feed your dog, for it may well be that the cause and prevention of bloat or flatulence lies here.

Another condition often experienced, which is more of an annoyance than a worry, is bad ears. The dog frequently shakes his head, and in neglected cases the ends of the ears become sore and bleeding. A simple solution of one part of flowers of sulphur mixed with three parts of liquid paraffin, used weekly to gently clean the inside base of the ear, will completely eliminate this nuisance. The treatment is so inexpensive that it is an excellent idea to completely lubricate the ear flap with the solution at the same time, thus keeping it supple and soft.

Skin complaints are not often seen in the breed, although common mange (sarcoptic mange) can easily be caught from other dogs, from unclean benches and from fleas and lice from the bedding of infected animals. Mange can develop slowly or very rapidly, and is not always recognisable. The dog scratches incessantly, and a loss of hair occurs. It is highly contagious, and a cure can only be brought about by absolute cleanliness and use of the necessary medicated baths and lotions which your vet will supply once he has diagnosed the condition. Treatment is simple and effective, and this skin complaint should disappear within a few weeks. Although not very serious, it can be annoying, and is sometimes persistent and hard to clear. It is communicable to the human being but has a limited effect from two to three weeks.

Some Great Danes seem prone to knock the ends of their tails, usually the happy dog who in his excitement is quite likely to damage the tip. Unfortunately this can become tiresome, for the constant wagging aggravates and enlarges the open place. In severe cases, the end of the tail may be amputated to achieve a complete cure, but this rather spoils the dog if he is required for future show purposes, so do not resort to this decision until all else has failed. The damaged end must be dressed daily and well bandaged with plenty of padding to protect the injured area. It is a long and painstaking job to heal a damaged tail, but the cure can be successful and permanent. In the final stages the skin thickens into a hard corn or callous and there is no further need to worry, but this stage is not reached without perseverance.

No one likes fights, and the ideal thing is to avoid them. But where they do occur and there are injuries, cut the hair away around the affected area and thoroughly wash with a mild antiseptic or a solution of salt and water—one teaspoonful to the pint. In the case of severe injuries consult your vet immediately, for stitching may be necessary and injections of penicillin required.

Milk fever (known as eclampsia) is associated with whelping and lactation, and can occur at any time during the period when a bitch is nursing her litter. In the early stages she appears restless and worried and the puppies may also become discontented. Later, the bitch may collapse and have convulsions, and prompt veterinary attention is necessary to avoid death. Treatment is by means of calcium injections, and if taken in time a complete cure can be effected. After-care is of great importance, for there may be a recurrence of this condition.

We have never experienced this illness in our kennels, and it can be prevented where an adequate diet of milk and other calcium-rich foods is given to the bitch in whelp, following through her nursing of the litter.

Eczema is a skin disease which is occasionally encountered, but in most cases the root cause is found to be dietary. Wet eczema can appear literally overnight: the infected area has the appearance of a large, wet sore, which exudes moisture, a crust-like surface forms and the hair disappears. Patches more often appear at the root of the tail, along the back and behind the ears. The cause may not always be obvious, but it is more frequently seen in the summer and it may be that fleas and lice can act as an irritant. The strange thing is, however, that what causes wet eczema in one dog does not affect another.

A complete change of diet will sometimes effect a quick cure, if allied to local treatment. Dogs regularly fed on meat and biscuits should be changed to milk and fish for a few days, and a half-teaspoon of Epsom Salts sprinkled over the food once a day will cleanse the blood. The dog should also be given a medicated bath, followed a few days later by another. If recovery is not rapid, consult your vet.

In cases of dry eczema the skin becomes rough and reddened, and can in some instances turn black. The hair becomes thin and broken, and sometimes the true cause is demodectic. Treatment should be as for wet eczema, but here again seek veterinary advice if there is not a rapid improvement.

At one time entropion (more often referred to as 'ingrowing eyelids') was not uncommon in Great Danes. This is an hereditary condition which can cause constant irritation to the dog; the eyelids and lashes turn in onto the eyes, which constantly exude a watery or other discharge. If allowed to continue, a serious condition can result in the eye becoming ulcerated, leading to eventual blindness. A minor operation will correct the trouble, but it should be fully appreciated that animals with entropion should *not* be bred from *under any circumstances*, for there is a real risk that the fault will be perpetuated.

Fits and hysteria no longer occur so frequently as in the past. Hysteria causes the dog to race madly around, blindly crashing into any object which happens to be in the way, frequently injuring himself and finally collapsing in an exhausted state. It was thought at one time that the agene in white flour was responsible for hysteria, but it is seldom experienced nowadays and mainly affects puppies, which eventually grow out of it and seem none the worse.

Fits can be caused by a variety of reasons: teething, worms and distemper can all be contributory causes. The indications are that the dog suddenly collapses, with jaws clamped together and the limbs extended and rigid. He froths at the mouth, the bladder and bowels may be emptied involuntarily, and he 'paddles' his front feet and cries out. When consciousness returns he appears dazed, and full vision may not be regained straight away. Keep the dog warm and completely quiet in a darkened room following a fit, and in the meantime seek veterinary advice in order that the cause can be diagnosed.

Most owners find their dog with a stomach upset at some time or another. This may be only a mild form which clears up quickly, or possibly the more serious condition of gastro-enteritis. A straightforward stomach disorder will probably respond to a day's starvation and then a slow return to normal diet; in this type of case the dog is likely to have loose motions but is not generally off-colour in himself.

Gastro-enteritis is a much more serious illness in which there is vomiting and diarrhoea, possibly accompanied by a rise in temperature. An infection of this kind can make rapid progress in a puppy or adult, and in a matter of hours a dog can be reduced from first-class health to near death, for one of the problems is complete dehydration. This condition needs prompt attention: the animal should be isolated in a warm, dry kennel, and with correct and speedy treatment should quickly return to health. Great care should be taken in these cases, for it may be that the illness is indicative of a virus infection, and if not promptly dealt with could spread through a kennel like wildfire.

Parvovirus is a very serious virus which shows itself in the form of acute enteritis and often proves fatal in puppies and older dogs. It is considered a new disease in dogs, as the veterinary profession first became aware of it in the late seventies. It was recognized officially in 1980 and given the name of parvovirus. It is now possible to inoculate dogs and young puppies but, as yet, the term of protection cannot be guaranteed and it is advisable to consult your veterinary surgeon as to when boosters should be recommended. Most vets like to boost puppies at eighteen weeks.

Growths of both benign and malignant type may affect the older dog in particular, but in all cases immediate expert advice should be sought. Cancer of the bone has been known in Great Danes, the dog first becoming lame and then the whole leg swelling until he is finally in great pain. However, for the number of dogs bred I would say the incidence of bone cancer is very low indeed.

Hepatitis is a specific virus infection, but there is a most effective inoculation against this which should be given when the puppies are vaccinated against hardpad and distemper. The disease can pursue a rapid and fatal course, especially in puppies. In adults it may show itself in a mild form, with no symptoms other than a tummy upset which may be followed some days later by the appearance of a blue film on the surface of the eyes.

Hiccups, frequently seen in puppies, are not in any way serious, and usually occur after meals. They may sometimes indicate that a puppy is not free from worms, and in this case it is advisable to administer a worm dosage if this has not been given for some weeks.

Hip dysplasia has become a talking point in most breeds today. This is an hereditary malformation of the hip joints, and in severe cases lameness is apparent. The last veterinary survey in the United Kingdom showed the Great Dane to be 'free', but the utmost care should always be taken when selecting breeding stock to ensure that it is particularly strong in quarters and sound in movement.

Another worry you may encounter is jaundice. Cleanliness is the important factor here, for in badly managed kennels the urine of infected carrier dogs and rats can be responsible. Again, prevention is better than cure, and preventive inoculations may be given when you first have your puppy.

With the nursing bitch mastitis is not uncommon. Make a regular point of feeling the glands under the bitch each time you attend to her throughout the day. Mastitis can quite suddenly appear, when one of the glands becomes infected, the puppies no longer take off the milk and a hard lump is formed. Hot fomentations should be applied and the milk drawn off, and if the condition does not respond quickly antibiotics may be necessary. This can all too easily develop into a chronic condition, and if an abscess forms the bitch cannot continue to feed her puppies.

Metritis is an inflammation of the uterus, and is an infection with a number of causes. Variable symptoms are likely, but generally there is dirty discharge from the bitch which has a putrid smell. Expert advice should be quickly sought.

Nephritis is a disease of the kidneys which accounts for many premature deaths among dogs; again, the complete vaccination is a safeguard against the main risk. With this illness, the dog shows great thirst and loss of condition, and the breath smells 'fishy'. In acute cases there is vomiting and back pains, accompanied by a rise in temperature. The diet must be altered to contain very little protein, and small meals should be taken regularly. Barley water should be substituted for ordinary water, and can be made as follows: one pint of boiling water, two large tablespoons of pearl barley stirred together, and allowed to cool, and strained.

Fleas and lice are common parasites with which most dogs come into contact during their lifetime, although regular weekly dusting with a Gammexine powder product is a good precaution. These parasites are known to carry the intermediate stage of the tapeworm, and for this reason alone it is important to keep the dogs as free as possible.

Harvest mites can be found in chalky areas between July and October, and appear as clusters of minute reddish-orange dots close to the skin, mainly between the toes and the ear pockets. They cause severe irritation, but a medicated bath will usually bring relief and clear the condition. As always, however, be guided by your vet.

Roundworms are common in puppies, and adult dogs may also be affected from time to time. These are white in colour and round in cross-section, being pointed at both ends and varying in length from ½ in. to 3 in. One particular form of roundworm can be passed to the puppies from their dam before birth. As a matter of routine, bitches should be wormed before or soon after mating, and all breeding stock should be wormed at least twice a year. Symptoms of the presence of roundworms can be loss of condition and diarrhoea, and in young puppies pot belly is also indicative of infestation. Worm the dog with an approved preparation—Antoban obtained from your vet is one of the best remedies. It is important to weigh the dogs and dose accurately, then repeat the dose a week to ten days later. Far too many puppies have worms, so it is really imperative that they should be wormed at approximately a month. Unless they are cleared of the worms their growth may be severely retarded. Rickets can also be attributed to neglect in worming young stock.

Tapeworms are not so common, but can be stubborn to eradicate. They are flat in cross-section and consist of many small segments, some of which can be seen in a dog's motion. They are not passed from dog to dog, but spend part of their life-cycle in the flea, louse and rabbit, hence the wisdom of keeping your dogs free from fleas and lice. With tapeworms the dog has a dull 'staring' coat, and is generally out of condition; he sometimes becomes very thin, but this is not always the case, and dogs which are carrying excess weight can also have a tapeworm. Dose strictly according to directions. Following dosing it is very important to make sure that the actual head of the worm is passed in the dog's motions—only then can you be certain that the trouble is cleared.

Hookworms and whipworms are not encountered very often in this country. The symptoms are not generally obvious to the layman, and it is only by the testing of motions that they can be detected. There is frequently no general debility, so it is important that veterinary advice is sought and expert treatment given.

Phantom pregnancies often occur in bitches of all ages—this condition usually arises at that period of the season when the bitch should be near to whelping even though she may not have been mated. Towards this time, i.e. at nine weeks, when she should be expecting her puppies, she will show all the usual signs of whelping such as enlargement and swelling of the mammary glands which may contain milk. At the time when she should actually whelp, she may go off her food and make her bed, all pointers to an imminent litter. A phantom pregnancy can last up to eight weeks if not checked, and affected bitches have been known to foster a litter and rear the puppies, which is most convenient if one is in need of a foster mother at that particular time. Treatment consists of cutting down the bitch's fluids, reducing her red meat ration to fish and white meat, and giving one teaspoon of Epsom Salts daily with the main meal. If the condition does not clear after a week, seek professional advice, for a more serious illness may arise as a result of neglect.

Some people believe that where a bitch has a tendency to false pregnancies, the complete remedy will lie in breeding a litter from her. This is not so: in cases where such a bitch has been bred from, she is quite likely to revert to phantom pregnancies in the future.

Occasionally a dog may have access to poison which will cause immediate harm and possible death. In these days of numerous insecticides, weed killers, slug poisons and so on, there is always a risk that dogs may come into contact with these dangers. A vet must be consulted at once, for it is essential to have immediate attention. Meantime, it will do no harm in most cases to encourage the dog to vomit, and this may be achieved by administering a piece of common washing soda about the size of a pea or hazel nut; this will act as a quick, first-aid emetic. If you telephone your vet, he can usually give you any essential information, and possibly advise the correct antidote and how best to deal with the situation until he arrives.

Rat poisons can also be fatal if not dealt with promptly. One well-known product which induces haemorrhage may only require vitamin K injections which cause the blood to clot correctly once more. Again, attention must be speedy.

Burning and scalding are accidents which may happen, in which case use Acriflavine as a first-aid measure. If injuries are severe, call the vet. There is a likelihood of shock, so keep the dog quiet and warm. Remain on the watch for several days, as severe burn symptoms are sometimes delayed.

We are fortunate that in this country the only poisonous snake we have is the adder, and these are generally found on heathy areas, usually during a hot summer. Adder bites are seldom fatal, but can be serious and should be attended to without delay by a vet. Immediate first-aid treatment is to cut the hair round the region of the bite, and then rub on crystals of potassium permanganate.

Bee and wasp stings happen quite often. With the former, the sting is usually left in and must be removed with tweezers. Apply an alkali such as washing soda (dissolve one teaspoon of washing soda in a teacup of water) or bicarbonate of soda (made up in a similar solution) to the sting area with cotton wool. Treat wasp stings with a weak acid such as vinegar and a cut lemon. When the dog is stung in the region of the throat or mouth it is dangerous and can prove fatal. Immediate first aid is a raw onion rubbed on the infected part, but the dog should be taken to a vet as soon as possible.

It is not always appreciated that dogs suffer from many of the diseases which also affect humans: pneumonia, various forms of heart disease, diseases of the kidney, and cancer in all its forms. Diabetes is not uncommon. Chronic nephritis—so well known to us—which causes the kidneys to gradually fail and eventually to cease functioning altogether, is also not infrequent.

I am often asked what is the average life-span of a Great Dane, and this is a difficult question to answer. Undoubtedly the larger breeds do not reach the great ages we know of in the small breeds, but Great Danes frequently live to be ten and eleven years old, and I did hear of one which reached the ripe old age of fifteen.

When the sad day comes and your old pal has to be put to sleep, stay with him. Veterinary surgeons are kindly people, and the method of destruction used nowadays is nothing more than the prick of a needle. If you are with him he will not be in the least alarmed or worried, and it is a small service to offer in farewell to an old and trusted friend.

POST-WAR KENNEL CLUB REGISTRATIONS

1948 —	639	1967 —	1504
1949 —	604	1968 —	1727
1950 —	540	1969 —	2140
1951 —	476	1970 —	2174
1952 —	305	1971 —	1999
1953 —	311	1972 —	2310
1954 —	331	1973 —	2500
1955 —	265	1974 —	2330
1956 —	398	1975 —	1953
1957 —	425	1976 —	1953
1958 —	462	1977 —	872
1959 —	519	1978 —	595
1960 —	569	1979 —	1552
1961 —	723	1980 —	2519
1962 —	893	1981 —	2812
1963 —	898	1982 —	2381
1964 —	967	1983 —	2255
1965 —	1170	1984 —	2555
1966 —	1223	1985 —	2432

The registration system of the Kennel Club went through a fundamental change in 1976. As from 1 April of that year the format was revised. With the tremendous increase in the number of pure-bred dogs in the United Kingdom, it had become necessary to develop the current system which involves the recording of each litter and the number of puppies. Dogs which may eventually be shown and bred from may then be registered into the active list with a recorded name.

GREAT DANE SPECIALIST CLUBS

The Great Dane Breeders' Association
The Great Dane Club
The Midland and West Great Dane Club
The Northern Great Dane Club
The Scottish Great Dane Club
The Irish Great Dane Club
The South-Western Great Dane Club

The names and addresses of secretaries of the above clubs may be obtained from the Secretary of the Kennel Club, 1 Clarges Street, Piccadilly, London W1Y 8AB (Telephone: 01–493–6651).

071 6295828

POST-WAR CHAMPIONS

Year	Name	Sex	Birth	Colour	Sire	Dam	Owner	Breeder
1945	Nil							
1946	Nil							
1947	Nil							—
1948	Juan of Winome	D	24-6-44	F	Bafflino of Blendon	Brindle Lady of Winome	Mrs E. C. Rowberry	Capt. & Mrs Rowberry
1948	Royalism of Ouborough	D	15-7-45	F	Raffles of Ouborough	Rezhitsa of Ouborough	Mr J. V. Rank	Mr J. V. Rank
1948	Bon Adventure of Barvae	B	10-1-46	F	Rebellion of Ouborough	Bridesmaid of Barvae	Mrs G. M. Clayton	Mrs G. M. Clayton
1949	Frost of the Wideskies	D	8-1-46	H	Storm of the Wideskies	Mist of the Wideskies	Miss M. Lomas	Miss M. Lomas
1949	Jillida of Winome	B	13-5-46	F	Rebellion of Ouborough	Juno of Winome	Mrs. E. C. Rowberry	Mrs E. C. Rowberry
1949	Raet of Ouborough	B	15-4-46	Br	Ch. Royalism of Ouborough	Ch. Ryot of Ouborough	Mr J. V. Rank	Mrs C. R. Robb
1949	Rusa of Ouborough	B	4-3-45	F	Rebellion of Ouborough	Rola of Ouborough	Mr J. V. Rank	Mr J. V. Rank

Year	Name	Sex	Birth	Colour	Sire	Dam	Owner	Breeder
1949	Ryot of Ouborough	B	4-3-45	Br	Rebellion of Ouborough	Rola of Ouborough	Mrs C. R. Robb	Mr J. V. Rank
1950	Basra of Bringtonhill	D	23-6-44	F	Hyperion of Ladymeade	Black Beauty of Brington	Mrs W. R. Ennals	Mrs W. R. Ennals
1950	Revert of Ouborough	D	19-10-45	F	Rilon Wilverly Romeo	Rubye of Ouborough	Mrs E. J. Allen	Mr J. V. Rank
1950	Dawnlight of Ickford	D	28-11-47	F	Ch. Royalism of Ouborough	Radiance of Ladymeade	Mrs M. S. Laming	Mrs M. S. Laming
1950	Rivolet of Ouborough	D	26-3-46	F	Rebellion of Ouborough	Jessica of Winome	Mr W. G. Siggers	Mr W. Thorp
1950	Banshee of Bringtonhill	B	9-5-47	Bl	Bahram of Bringtonhill	Black Beauty of Brington	Mrs W. R. Ennals	Mrs W. R. Ennals
1950	Jezebel of Winome	B	13-9-47	F	Blendons Fingards King of Kings	Juno of Winome	Mrs R. D. S. Main	Mrs E. C. Rowberry
1950	Rindel of Ouborough	B	15-4-47	Br	Ch. Royalism of Ouborough	Ch. Ryot of Ouborough	Mr J. V. Rank	Mrs C. R. Robb
1951	Jeep of Winome	D	13-9-47	F	Blendons Fingards King of Kings	June of Winome	Mrs E. C. Rowberry	Mrs E. C. Rowberry
1951	Penelope of Alderwasley	B	15-8-47	Br	Rambert of Ouborough	Bitter Sweet of Barvae	Mr & Mrs A. Perry	Mrs M. Perry
1952	Cloud of the Wideskies	D	6-4-45	H	Storm of the Wideskies	Dusk of the Wideskies	Miss M. Lomas	Miss M. Lomas

Year	Name		Date		Sire	Dam	Breeder	Owner
1952	Anndae Royal Light of Ickford	D	28-11-47	F	Ch. Royalism of Ouborough	Radiance of Ladymeade	Mr J. W. L. McKee	Mrs M. S. Laming
1952	Bonhomie of Blendon	D	23-12-49	Br	Bonheur of Blendon	Jhelum of Winome	Miss H. M. Osborn	Miss H. M. Osborn
1952	Deucher of Rynallen	D	1-1-48	F	Ch. Royalism of Ouborough	Reck of Ouborough	Miss L. B. Farquharson	Miss L. B. Farquharson
1952	Relate of Ouborough	D	21-2-50	F	Relec of Ouborough	Ch. Raet of Ouborough	Mr J. V. Rank	Mr J. V. Rank
1952	Baffleur of Blendon	B	17-3-48	F	Fingards King of Kings of Blendon	Baflette of Blendon	Mr Gordon Stewart	Miss H. M. Osborn
1952	Berynthia of Blendon	B	17-3-48	F	Fingards King of Kings of Blendon	Baflette of Blendon	Miss H. M. Osborn	Miss H. M. Osborn
1952	Rhagodia of Ouborough	B	16-8-48	F	Ch. Royalism of Ouborough	Blenda Flicka von Langenhof	Mr J. V. Rank	Mr A. M. Kuhn
1953	Elch Edler of Ouborough	D	26-4-51	F	Kalandus of Ouborough	Ch. Raet of Ouborough	Mr W. G. Siggers	Mr J. V. Rank
1953	Marfre Modern Ransom	D	7-8-49	F	Ch. Royalism of Ouborough	Bambi of Ouborough	Mrs M. Jones	Mrs J. McArthur Rank
1953	Imogen of Oldmanor	B	27-1-50	Br	Oldmanor Joyalism of Winome	Dainty of Oldmanor	Rev. & Mrs J. G. Davies	Mrs C. & Miss O. Russell
1953	Tandye of Moonsfield	B	5-9-48	F	Ch. Royalism of Ouborough	Tango of Moonsfield	Mrs E. M. Harrild	Mrs E. M. Harrild
1953	Vegar of Ouborough	B	23-2-47	Br	Marfre Danilo	Rezhitsa of Ouborough	Mrs I. B. Jones	Mr J. V. Rank

Year	Name	Sex	Birth	Colour	Sire	Dam	Owner	Breeder
1954	Boniface of Blendon	D	1-6-51	F	Ch. Bonhomie of Blendon	Berynthia of Blendon	Miss H. M. Osborn	Miss H. M. Osborn
1954	Festival of Ouborough	D	19-9-50	F	Kalandus of Ouborough	Ch. Raet of Ouborough	Mr L. E. Jacobs	Mr J. V. Rank
1955	Blackjack of Bringtonhill	D	11-4-51	Bl	Ch. Dawnlight of Ickford	Ch. Banshee of Bringtonhill	Mrs R. W. Ennals	Mrs R. W. Ennals
1955	Brin Cezar of Barvae	D	2-12-50	Br	Brindsley of Blendon	Ch. Bon Adventure of Barvae	Mr R. Wilkinson	Mrs G. M. Clayton
1955	Bronx of Blendon	D	21-7-48	F	Brandy of Blendon	Deborah of Blundell	Miss H. M. Osborn	Mr J. B. Scuffman
1955	Racketeer of Foxbar	D	5-5-50	Br	Ch. Royalism of Ouborough	Ch. Ryot of Ouborough	Mrs C. R. Robb	Mrs C. R. Robb
1955	Marfre Modern Miss	B	26-9-51	F	Ch. Marfre Modern Ransom	Ch. Rindel of Ouborough	Mrs M. S. Jones	Mrs C. R. Robb
1955	Rhapsody of Foxbar	B	26-9-51	Br	Ch. Marfre Modern Ransom	Ch. Rindel of Ouborough	Mrs E. M. Harrild	Mrs C. R. Robb
1956	Challenger of Clausentum	D	15-6-53	F	Ch. Bronx of Blendon	Claire of Clausentum	Mrs H. A. & Miss J. M. Lanning	Mrs H. A. & Miss J. M. Lanning
1956	Baroness of Coxdown	B	19-4-53	F	Ch. Elch Edler of Ouborough	Cleopatra of Coxdown	Miss D. V. Harding	Miss D. V. Harding
1956	Flambonetta of Billil	B	22-1-53	F	Ch. Bronx of Blendon	Flamusine of Billil	Miss J. I. Cameron	Mrs L. Isaac

1956	Surtees of Leesthorphill	D	8-9-50	H	Ch. Cloud of the Wideskies	Snow of the Wideskies	Mrs J. Kelly	Mrs J. Kelly
1957	Benign of Blendon	D	14-4-54	Br	Ch. Bronx of Blendon	Bethanie of Blendon	Miss H. M. Osborn	Miss H. M. Osborn
1957	Barilla of Ashthorpe	B	30-10-52	F	Aurorus of Rorydale	Khumbirgram Attraction	Mrs W. Atkin	Mrs J. Drinkwater
1957	Rhythm of Foxbar	B	26-9-51	Br	Ch. Marfre Modern Ransom	Ch. Rindel of Ouborough	Mr W. G. Siggers	Mrs C. R. Robb
1958	Telluson of Moonsfield	D	2-6-56	F	Tellus of Moonsfield	Merrie of Merrowlea	Mrs E. M. Harrild	Mr W. Page
1958	Bequest of Blendon	D	12-6-55	Br	Ch. Bonhomie of Blendon	Ch. Imogen of Oldmanor	Miss H. M. Osborn	Rev. & Mrs J. G. Davies
1958	Dawn of the Wideskies	B	3-2-54	H	Halo of the Wideskies	Madonna of the Wideskies	Mr L. Rose	Miss M. Lomas
1958	Enchantment of Yalding	B	18-4-54	F	Ch. Boniface of Blendon	Lady Suzette of Miriel	Mrs E. Cadbury-Brown	Mrs M. W. Hampshire
1958	Minuet of Oldmanor	B	12-6-55	F	Ch. Bonhomie of Blendon	Ch. Imogen of Oldmanor	Rev. & Mrs J. G. Davies	Rev. & Mrs J. G. Davies
1959	Bonifleur of Blendon	B	5-8-57	F	Bonifino of Blendon	Bronfleur of Blendon	Miss H. M. Osborn	Miss H. M. Osborn
1959	Squire of Ridgedaine	D	29-10-54	F	Ch. Elch Edler of Ouborough	Rux of Ouborough	Miss J. P. Prentis	Miss J. P. Prentis
1959	Isobelle of Ashtrees	B	10-5-54	F	Ch. Elch Elder of Ouborough	Modern Ranger	Mr J. & Miss L. E. Jackson	Mr. J. & Miss L. E. Jackson

Year	Name	Sex	Birth	Colour	Sire	Dam	Owner	Breeder
1959	Marquise of Hornsgreen	B	8-10-55	Bl	Bahni of Bringtonhill	Newtonregis Belle	Major & Mrs M. P. McFarland	Mrs N. Rowe
1959	Tellus of Moonsfield	D	29-7-54	F	Ch. Elch Edler of Ouborough	Ch. Rhapsody of Foxbar	Mrs E. M. Harrild	Mrs E. M. Harrild
1959	Bonaida of Barvae	B	15-9-54	Br	Vulpus von Schloss Dellwig	Bon Viva of Barvae	Mr & Mrs M. S. Green	Mrs G. M. Clayton
1959	Bel Ami of Nightsgift	D	7-3-55	F	Ch. Bonhomie of Blendon	Ch. Flambonetta of Bilil	Miss J. C. Cameron	Miss J. C. Cameron
1960	Todhunter of Moonsfield	D	12-10-58	F	Ch. Telluson of Moonsfield	Taral of Moonsfield	Mrs M. S. Jones	Mrs E. M. Harrild
1960	Busaco of Blendon	D	5-9-57	Br	Bonifino of Blendon	Bronfleur of Blendon	Miss H. M. Osborn	Miss H. M. Osborn
1960	Sutton of Leesthorphill	D	14-5-56	H	Ch. Surtees of Leesthorphill	Sucan of Leesthorphill	Mrs J. Kelly	Mrs J. Kelly
1960	Moyra of Oldmanor	B	1-11-56	Br	Oldmanor Brand of Bringtonhill	Ch. Imogen of Oldmanor	Rev. & Mrs J. G. Davies	Rev. & Mrs J. G. Davies
1961	Banquet of Blendon	D	31-3-58	Br	Ch. Bequest of Blendon	Carousel of Clounaye	Mrs N. Hanson	Mrs B. Sherman
1961	Blendon Apollo of Coldash	D	5-1-58	F	Ch. Boniface of Blendon	Vels Vanity	Miss H. M. Osborn	Mrs A. B. Pope
1961	Hampton of Ridgedaine	D	26-11-55	F	Brinsley of Barvae	Cinnamon of Ridgedaine	Miss J. P. Prentis	Miss J. P. Prentis

Year	Name		Date		Sire	Dam	Owner	Owner
1961	Hyperbole of Ouborough	D	7-11-58	F	Sabre of Horsebridge	Etfa of Ouborough	Mr W. G. Siggers	Mr W. G. Siggers
1961	Telton of Moonsfield	D	26-4-56	F	Ch. Tellus of Moonsfield	Twinstar of Moonsfield	Mrs E. M. Harrild	Mrs E. M. Harrild
1961	Minuet Miss of Oldmanor	B	24-12-57	F	Ch. Bequest of Blendon	Ch. Minuet of Oldmanor	Rev. & Mrs J. G. Davies	Rev. & Mrs J. G. Davies
1962	Benison of Blendon	D	3-12-58	F	Ch. Benign of Blendon	Bronfleur of Blendon	Miss H. M. Osblm	Miss H. M. Osborn
1962	Saturn of Nightsgift	D	7-3-60	F	Benjamin of Newtonregis	Bonetta of Nightsgift	Miss J. Cameron	Miss J. Cameron
1962	Survey of Leesthorphill	D	15-2-59	H	Ch. Surtees of Leesthorphill	Leesthorphill Nugget of Gold of Limes	Mrs J. Kelly	Mrs J. Kelly
1962	Seranda of Leesthorphill	B	17-9-57	H	Seagull of Leesthorphill	Nugget of Gold of the Limes	Mrs J. Kelly	Mrs J. Kelly
1962	Tapestry of Moonsfield	B	24-3-58	Br	Ch. Bequest of Blendon	Twinstar of Moonsfield	Mr H. V. Harrild	Mrs E. M. Harrild
1962	Surcelle of Leesthorphill	B	15-2-59	H	Ch. Surtees of Leesthorphill	Nugget of Gold of the Limes	Mrs J. Kelly	Mrs J. Kelly
1962	Penruddock Eslilda	B	10-10-56	Br	Flamatelot of Billil	Penruddock Esmeralda	Mrs D. K. F. Peck	Mrs D. K. F. Peck
1963	Archie of Arranton	D	2-12-60	F	Arab of Arranton	Kerensa of Ashthorpe	Mr & Mrs S. A. Green	Mr A. Wildman
1963	Malloy of Merrowlea	D	12-12-59	F	My Choice of Merrowlea	Marilon of Merrowlea	Miss P. M. Rossiter	Mrs J. Toye

Year	Name	Sex	Birth	Colour	Sire	Dam	Owner	Breeder
1963	Moyalism of Oldmanor	D	4-10-59	Br	Oldmanor Tattoo of Moonsfield	Ch. Moyra of Oldmanor	Rev. & Mrs J. G. Davies	Rev. & Mrs J. G. Davies
1963	Goldendale Gay of Merrowlea	B	3-6-57	F	Ch. Squire of Ridgedaine	Genevieve of Goldendale	Mr E. J. Hutton	Mrs G. Harrison
1963	Soraya of Nightsgift	B	20-2-59	F	Ch. Tellus of Moonsfield	Ch. Flambonetta of Bilil	Miss J. Cameron	Miss J. Cameron
1964	Milady of Hornsgreen	B	24-8-59	Bl	Black Banner of Blendon	Ch. Marquise of Hornsgreen	Mr D. Hewlett	Major & Mrs. M. P. MacFarland
1964	Bullington Corneille	D	11-2-61	F	Bullinton Algenon of Arranton	Flamunity of Bilil	Mr & Mrs Bryn-Jones	Mrs J. Makin
1964	Telaman of Moonsfield	D	23-1-62	F	Ch. Telluson of Moonsfield	Taral of Moonsfield	Mrs E. M. Harrild	Mrs E. M. Harrild
1964	Anne of Arranton	B	2-12-60	F	Arab of Arranton	Kerensa of Ashthorpe	Mr & Mrs S. A. Green	Mr A. Wildman
1964	Surice of Leesthorphill	B	11-1-52	H	Ch. Sutton of Leesthorphill	Ch. Survey of Leesthorphill	Mrs J. Kelly	Mrs J. Kelly
1965	Arex of Arranton	D	4-2-62	F	Arab of Arranton	Kerensa of Ashthorpe	Mr & Mrs S. A. Green	Mr A. Wildman
1965	Merrymonk of Merrowlea	D	2-10-61	F	Ch. Malloy of Merrowlea	Ch. Goldendale Gay of Merrowlea	Capt & Mrs E. J. Hutton	Capt E. J. Hutton
1965	Amalia of Arranton	B	17-2-60	Br	Oldmanor Tattoo of Moonsfield	Aida of Arranton	Mr & Mrs S. A. Green	Mrs L. Edsall

Year	Name		Date		Sire	Dam	Breeder	Owner
1965	Billil Tres Bon of Moonsfield	B	30-7-61	F	Ch. Telluson of Moonsfield	Tellona of Moonsfield	Mrs L. Isaac	Mrs E. M. Harrild
1965	Walkmyll Moonyean of Edzell	B		F	Oldmanor Tattoo of Moonsfield	Aida of Arranton	Mrs F. C. Lewis	Mrs L. Edsall
1965	Tayntemead Tamsee of Moonsfield	B	20-2-60	Br	Vanburgh of Clartay	Dunbracken Gardrum Morag	Mrs A. E. Spencer	Miss E. Niven
1965	Hatchmead Pericles of Nightsgift	D	13-6-61	F	Ch. Saturn of Nightsgift	Ch. Soraya of Nightsgift	Mrs J. Thomas	Miss J. Cameron
1966	Mason of Edzell	D	15-6-63	Br	Arrand of Arranton	Amber Light of Ancholme	Mr & Mrs P. V. K. Edsall	Mrs Atkins
1966	Moretime of Merrowlea	D	21-2-61	F	Sabre of Horsebridge	Musical Lyric of Merrowlea	Mr A. S. Cormack	Mrs E. M. Nobbs
1966	Mr Softee of Merrowlea	D	18-10-62	F	Ch. Malloy of Merrowlea	Ch. Goldendale Gay of Merrowlea	Capt & Mrs E. J. Hutton	Capt. & Mrs E. J. Hutton
1966	Meleta of Oldmanor	B	4-5-62	F	Ch. Moyalism of Oldmanor	Minuet Maid of Oldmanor	Rev. & Mrs J. G. Davies	Rev. & Mrs J. G. Davies
1966	Sulia of Leesthorphill	B	11-8-64	H	Surrel of Leesthorphill	Sequence of Leesthorphill	Mrs J. Kelly	Mrs J. Kelly
1966	Madame of Merrowlea	B	18-11-60	F	Sultan of Ridgedaine	My Fair Lady of Merrowlea	Capt & Mrs E. J. Hutton	Mr F. G. Kinch
1966	Beechfield Buxom Wench of Texall	B	27-1-64	F	Oldmanor Brand of Bringtonhill	Caribbean Queen	Mrs B. Kirkman	Mr H. V. Anderson
1967	Merry Deal of Merrowlea	D	18-10-62	F	Ch. Malloy of Merrowlea	Ch. Goldendale Gay of Merrowlea	Capt & Mrs E. J. Hutton	Capt & Mrs E. J. Hutton

Year	Name	Sex	Birth	Colour	Sire	Dam	Owner	Breeder
1967	Buscilla of Blendon	B	11-10-63	Br	Ch. Busaco of Blendon	Banksia of Blendon	Miss H. M. Osborn	Miss H. M. Osborn
1967	Comtessa Fiona of Ouborough	B	23-6-63	Br	Quantas of Ouborough	Vila of Ouborough	Mr W. G. Siggers	Mr W. G. Siggers
1967	Oldmanor Pioneer of Daneii	D	26-2-64	F	Ch. Moyalism of Oldmanor	Mysore of Oldmanor	Rev. & Mrs J. G. Davies	Mr V. Fones
1967	Miss Fancy Free of Merrowlea	B	18-10-62	F	Ch. Malloy of Merrowlea	Ch. Goldendale Gay of Merrowlea	Capt & Mrs E. J. Hutton	Capt & Mrs E. J. Hutton
1967	My Mink of Merrowlea	B	26-7-62	F	Sabre of Horsebridge	Melia of Merrowlea	Mrs D. A. Oliver	Mrs D. A. Oliver
1967	Sawspitsville	D	26-4-64	F	Ch. Todhunter of Moonsfield	Benizora of Blendon	Mr J. W. Ellyatt	Major & Mrs Smither
1967	Clausentum Fenton of Fenbridge	D	23-9-65	F	Ch. Arex of Arranton	Jayessem Janice	Mrs H. A. & Miss J. M. Lanning	Mr W. Bishop
1967	Struth of Bringtonhill	D	29-11-66	F	Ch. Telaman of Moonsfield	Solitaire of Bringtonhill	Mrs E. Ennals	Mrs E. Ennals
1968	Astrid of Arranton	D	6-6-64	F	Ch. Telaman of Moonsfield	Ch. Anne of Arranton	Mrs J. Laing	Mr & Mrs A. Green
1968	Melba Messenger of Oldmanor	D	21-6-65	F	Ch. Oldmanor Pioneer of Daneii	Mimbelba of Oldmanor	Mrs V. N. Forrest	Rev & Mrs J. G. Davies
1968	Mighty Fine of Merrowlea	D	13-8-63	F	Ch. Malloy of Merrowlea	My Delight of Merrowlea	Mr R. Muir	Capt & Mrs E. J. Hutton

1968	Try Again of Moonsfield	B	12-3-62	F	Ch. Telton of Moonsfield	Ch. Tazana of Moonsfield	Mr & Mrs B. R. Round	Mrs E. M. Harrild
1969	Best Man of Blendon	D	20-11-66	Br	Bridegroom of Blendon	Oonah of Belregis	Miss Osborn & Mrs Birchmore	Mrs O. Bell
1969	Candy of Walkmyll	B	22-10-65	Br	Ch. Moyalism of Oldmanor	Ch. Walkmyll Moonyean of Edzell	Mrs F. C. Lewis	Mrs F. C. Lewis
1969	Meletalyon of Oldmanor	D	6-12-66	F	Ch. Telaman of Moonsfield	Ch. Meleta of Oldmanor	Rev. & Mrs J. G. Davies	Rev. & Mrs J. G. Davies
1969	Merry Melba of Oldmanor	B	16-1-66	F	Ch. Oldmanor Pioneer of Daneii	Mimelba of Oldmanor	Rev. & Mrs J. G. Davies	Rev. & Mrs J. G. Davies
1969	Myabella of Oldmanor	B	31-5-66	F	Ch. Oldmanor Pioneer of Daneii	Moyahiti of Oldmanor	Mrs M. White	Rev. & Mrs J. G. Davies
1969	Sherelake Storm-Crest of Blendon	D	15-10-64	F	Ch. Benison of Blendon	Sherelake Stormbird	Miss H. M. Osborn	Mr D. Spray
1969	Telera of Moonsfield	B	18-5-65	Br	Ch. Telton of Moonsfield	Neara of Tayntemead	Mrs E. M. Harrild	Mr J. Steel
1970	Fergus of Clausentum	D	28-12-67	F	Clausentum Danelaghs Quillan	Creole of Clausentum	Mra H. A. & Miss J. M. Lanning	Mrs H. A. & Miss J. M. Lanning
1970	Sarzec Blue Baron	D	3-10-65	B	Sarzec Blue Saxon	Kana of Kilcroney	Mr & Mrs D. Craig	Mr E. Walshe & Mrs J. Coyne
1970	My Ambition of Oldmanor	D	25-2-68	F	Ch. Meletalyon of Oldmanor	Missmanor of Oldmanor	Rev & Mrs J. G. Davies	Rev. & Mrs J. G. Davies
1970	Kaptain of Kilcroney	D	11-5-67	Bl	Ch. Moyalism of Oldmanor	Ir. Ch. Kara of Kilcroney	Mrs G. Le Coyne	Mrs G. Le Coyne

Year	Name	Sex	Birth	Colour	Sire	Dam	Owner	Breeder
1970	Gowerfield Candy Caress of Aysdaine	B	1-9-67	F	Ch. Oldmanor Pioneer of Daneii	Delilah of Aysdaine	Mr & Mrs A. Clement	Mrs A. B. Shepperd
1970	Miss Monica of Oldmanor	B	24-12-68	F	Ch. Oldmanor Pioneer of Daneii	Miss Barford of Oldmanor	Rev. & Mrs J. G. Davies	Rev. & Mrs J. G. Davies
1970	Muffettee of Oldmanor	B	18-8-65	F	Ch. Meletalyon of Oldmanor	Missmanor of Oldmanor	Rev. & Mrs J. G. Davies	Rev. & Mrs J. G. Davies
1971	Miss Freedom of Merrowlea	B	1-12-66	F	Ch. Merry Deal of Merrowlea	Miss Carefree of Merrowlea	Mr & Mrs K. Le Mare	Capt. & Mrs E. J. Hutton
1971	Steed of Bringtonhill	D	1-6-68	F	Ch. Telaman of Moonsfield	Solitair of Bringtonhill	Mrs N. Ennals	Mrs R. W. Ennals
1971	Gaylaing Astronaut	D	27-2-68	F	Ch. Sherelake Storm Crest of Blendon	Ch. Astrid of Aranton	Mrs J. A. Laing	Owner
1971	Lotus of Walkmyll	B	18-2-69	F	Ch. Bencaross Beau Brummel	Parabar Meriel	Mrs F. C. Lewis	Owner
1971	My Ben of Oldmanor	D	25-2-68	Br	Ch. Oldmanor Pioneer of Daneii	Margery of Oldmanor	Rev. & Mrs J. G. Davies	Owner
1971	Gowerfield Tartan Muse of Moonsfield	B	20-1-68	F	Ch. Telaman of Moonsfield	Tartan of Moonsfield	Mr A. Clemence	Mrs E. M. Harrild
1971	Merry Analyst of Oldmanor	D	15-12-68	F	Meletalyon of Oldmanor	Merry Melba of Oldmanor	Mr R. Primmer	Rev. & Mrs J. G. Davies
1971	Terrel of Moonsfield	B	13-3-68	F	Ch. Telaman of Moonsfield	Desdamona of Cheluth	Mrs E. Harrild	Mr Bellamy

1971	Timellie Caspian	D	11-7-69	F	Ch. Fergus of Clausentum	Timellie Cassandra	Mr & Mrs E. M. Harmes-Cooke	Breeder
1971	Mini Artful of Oldmanor	B	17-12-68	F	Ch. Oldmanor Pioneer of Daneii	Minimischief of Oldmanor	Mrs Doyne	Rev. & Mrs J. G. Davies
1971	Leesthorphill Sultan of Escheatlands	D	24-9-68	H	Ch. Surrel of Leesthorphill	Secret of Leesthorphill	Mrs J. Kelly	Dr M. Lloyd
1971	Malindi of Helmlake	B	14-1-70	F	Ch. Fergus of Clausentum	Ch. Miss Freedom of Merrowlea	Mrs K. Le Mare	Owner
1972	Laburmax Eurydice	B	24-11-68	F	Ch. Oldmanor Pioneer of Daneii	Aliandra of Ancholme	Mr A. Clemence	Mrs B. E. Price
1972	Wykendrift Marcellus	D	28-1-70	F	Ch. Gaylaing Astronaut	Radiant Roxanna of Nira	Miss B. E. Boustead	Owner
1972	Simba of Helmlake	D	14-1-70	F	Ch. Fergus of Clausentum	Ch. Miss Freedom of Merrowlea	Mrs K. Le Mare	Owner
1972	Dulcie of Harverdane	B	18-11-68	F	Dominic of Beechfields	Melba Merrie of Oldmanor	Mrs V. N. Forrest	Owner
1973	Impton Duralex Burnita	B	25-4-69	Bl	Nordic Ch. Harmony Hill Lied of Airways	Nordic Ch. Chansonette of Doggline	Mrs M. Everton	Mr & Mrs G. Pettersson
1973	Big Sur of Impton	D	4-5-70	Blue	Sarzec Blue Baron	Marpesa of Merrowlea	Mrs M. Everton	Mr & Mrs B. Everton
1973	Merry Muffin of Oldmanor	D	25-11-69	F	Ch. Meletalyon of Oldmanor	Ch. Merry Melba of Oldmanor	Mr. & Mrs. B. Draper	Rev. & Mrs J. G. Davies
1973	Impton Duralex Bernando	D	25-4-69	Bl	Nordic Ch. Harmony Hill Lied of Airways	Nordic Ch. Chansonette of Doggline	Mrs M. Everton	Mr & Mrs G. Pettersson

Year	Name	Sex	Birth	Colour	Sire	Dam	Owner	Breeder
1973	Helmlake Mahe	B	24-1-72	F	Simjea's Hamlet	Ch. Miss Freedom of Merrowlea	Mr & Mrs G. Le Mare	Owners
1973	Timellie My Cheerful	B	21-1-71	F	Timellie Cassius	Timellie Cheerful	Mrs E. M. Harmes-Cooke	Owner
1973	Walkmyll Kaster of Clausentum	D	20-6-69	F	Ch. Fergus of Clausentum	Jennifer of Clausentum	Mrs F. C. Lewis	Mrs H. A. & Miss J. M. Lanning
1974	Airways Wrangler of Impton	D	30-8-71	Br	Nordic Sh. Ch. Harmony Lied of Airways	Nordic Sh. Ch. Airways Lazy Susan	Mr & Mrs B. M. Everton	Ulla & Curt Magnusson
1974	Bellote Boffin	D	13-5-71	F	Gulliver of Taftan	Bellote Tendrill of Moonsfield	Mr & Mrs R. McHaffey	Owners
1974	Helmlake Chico	D	5-5-72	H	Helmlake Ben El Eick von Forellenparadies	Helmlake Magic Columbine of Merrowlea	Mr & Mrs G. Le Mare	Owners
1974	Impton Apache	D	25-11-72	Bl	Nordic Ch. Impton Duralex Bernando	Sierra of Impton	Mr & Mrs D. Van der Vyver	Mr & Mrs B. M. Everton
1974	Timellie Cheerleader	D	21-1-71	F	Timellie Cassius	Timellie Cheerful	Mrs V. Harms-Cooke	Owner
1974	Tyegarth Hamlet	D	11-4-69	F	Meletalyon of Oldmanor	Tyegarth Elsinore	Miss S. F. Cartwright	Owner
1974	Dicarl the Lioness of Jafrak	B	18-3-73	F	Ch. Simba of Helmlake	Dicarl Tarbaby	Mr & Mrs J. Krall	Mrs D. M. Johnson
1974	Gracelove Kinda Special	B	28-8-70	F	Gracelove Tinuss of Brookview	Gracelove My Answer of Oldmanor	Mrs H. & Miss K. Giles & Mrs E. Jones	Owners

Year	Name	Sex	Date	Sire	Dam	Breeder	Owner
1974	Helmlake Curieuse	B	24-1-72	Simjea's Hamlet	Ch. Miss Freedom of Merrowlea	Miss B. Sorensen	Mr & Mrs G. Le Mare
1974	Kontiki Coral Reef	B	22-7-71	Buccaneer of Beechfields	Kukara of Kontiki	Mr R. Marshall	Owner
1975	Gowerfield Gilden	D	2-9-72	Gowerfield Galeforce	Genie of Gowerfield	Mrs A. Heaton	Mr & Mrs A. Clement
1975	Helmlake Praslin	Br	24-1-72	Simjea's Hamlet	Ch. Miss Freedom of Merrowlea	Mr & Mrs G. Le Mare	Owners
1975	Walkmyll Storm	D	5-11-72	Ch. Walkmyll Kaster of Clausentum	Ch. Lotus of Walkmyll	Mrs F. C. Lewis	Owner
1975	Oldmanor Manthem of Auldmoor	B	7-10-72	Ch. Meletalyon of Oldmanor	My Design of Oldmanor	Mrs A. Harris	Rev. & Mrs J. S. Davies
1975	Oldmanor Maymirth of Dorneywood	B	31-5-72	Ch. Meletalyon of Oldmanor	Ch. Miss Monica of Oldmanor	Mr & Mrs Parish	Rev. & Mrs J. S. Davies
1975	Sabuki of Sherain for Bridalane	B	13-8-73	Sherain Saul	Gowerfield Garrod	Mrs J. Briggs	M. Griffiths
1975	Shamgret Kosmea	B	4-4-72	Robin of Clausentum	Shamgret Fatme vom Rhein River	Mr & Mrs W. T. Hale	Owners
1976	Clausentum Gulliver	D	9-3-74	Ch. Fergus of Clausentum	Hattie of Clausentum	Mr & Mrs J. Butcher & Mrs H. A. Lanning	Miss J. M. Lanning
1976	Clausentum Magnus	D	18-3-74	Ch. Fergus of Clausentum	Hanah of Clausentum	Mr & Mrs P. M. Howell and Miss J. Lanning	Miss J. M. Lanning

Year	Name	Sex	Birth	Colour	Sire	Dam	Owner	Breeder
1976	Dicarl the Heavyweight	D	3–11–73	F	Ch. Gowerfield Galestorm of Aysdaine	Dicarl Tardus	Mr R. Gretton	Mrs D. M. Johnson
1976	Gowerfield Galestorm of Aysdaine	D	25–7–71	F	Golden Reward of Lisvaine	Ch. Gowerfield Tartan Muse of Moonsfield	Mrs Sheppard	Mr & Mrs A. Clement
1976	The Weightlifter of Dicarl	D	30–8–75	F	Ch. Dicarl the Heavyweight	Dicarl the Lioness of Jafrak	Mrs D. M. Johnson	Mr & Mrs J. Krall
1976	Moonsfield Tellora	B	3–10–73	F	Oakhatch Carl of Moonsfield	Terrel of Moonsfield	Mrs I. Wheeler	Mrs E. M. Harrild
1976	Solveig of Helmlake	B	27–7–73	F	Ch. Simba of Helmlake	Franny of Clausentum	Mr & Mrs G. Le Mare	Mrs L. McCulloch
1976	Dorneywood Dahlia of Walkmyll	B	22–4–75	F	Ch. Storm of Walkmyll	Ch. Oldmanor Maymirth of Dorneywood	Mrs F. C. Lewis	Mr & Mrs D. Parish
1977	Queen of Carpenders of Vironey	B	6–6–73	F	Dashtanga Stroller of Bringtonhill	Barnsfield Lady Jane	Mrs V. E. Bishop	Mrs J. J. Wiggett
1977	Dicarl the Pacemaker of Meadvale	D	19–8–74	F	Dicarl Surprizin Stew	Dicarl Tarbaby	Mr P. Stevens	Mrs D. Johnson
1977	Graceloves Tomorrows Hope	D	23–7–73	Br	Target of Moonsfield	Gracelove Telatone of Moonsfield	Mrs Jones & Mrs Giles	Owners

1977	**Shamgret Beatrix**	B	25-2-75	Br	Shamgret Sascha	Shamgret Dagmar	Mr & Mrs W. Hale	Owners
1977	Bringtonhill Oraya	B	15-9-74	F	Golden Reward of Lisvane	Tawny of Bringtonhill	Mrs N. Ennals	Mr H. R. Hunt
1977	Walkmyll Duncan	D	3-6-74	F	Ch. Walkmyll Storm	Tamarisk of Walkmyll	Mrs F. Lewis	Owner
1977	Kontiki Sea Splendour	B	5-8-74	F	Int. Ch. Nord. Airways Wrangler of Impton	Ch. Kontiki Coral Reef	Mr Roy Marshall	Owner
1977	Auldmoor Astute	D	9-1-75	F	Int. Ch. Nord. Airways Wrangler of Impton	Ch. Auldmoor Mantehm of Oldmanor	Mrs Tilley	Mrs A. Harris
1977	Dunoir Cora	B	4-9-74	H	Ch. Helmlake Chico	Masnou Jacarena of Dunoir	Mr & Mrs J. Middleton	Owners
1977	Helmlake Fancy Fashion	B	25-7-75	H	Ch. Helmlake Chico	Bettina of Helmlake	Mr & Mrs G. Le Mare	Owners
1977	Brutondane Blonde	B	26-3-75	F	Gaylaing Astrolad of Brutondane	Walkmyll Serenade of Brutondane	Mrs J. Alford	Mrs J. Roberts
1978	Tarus Major Concession	D	7-1-76	F	Tarus Arandyke	Kazim Lysander	Mrs J. Wright	Owner
1978	Dorneywood Debonair	B	23-7-76	F	Ch. Clausentum Gulliver	Ch. Oldmanor Maymirth of Dorneywood	Mr & Mrs D. Parish	Owners

Year	Name	Sex	Birth	Colour	Sire	Dam	Owner	Breeder
1978	Ch. Aysdaine Lion	D	8-10-76	F	Ch. The Weightlifter of Dicarl	Aysdaine Lighting	Mrs A. Shepherd	Owner
1978	Dicarl the Prize Fighter	D	2-8-75	Br	Tresylyan Tudor Minstrel	Dicarl Muffahiti of Oldmanor	Mrs D. Johnson	Owner
1978	Halemoss Bettina of Walkmyll	B	28-8-75	F	Ch. Walkmyll Storm	Georlina Deena of Halemoss	Mrs F. Lewis	Mrs H. Briscoe
1978	Timellie Clovanna	B	24-10-72	F	Timellie Cassius	Timellie Clover	Mrs V. Harmes-Cooke	Owner
1978	Enydelet Pandora Beauty	B	22-10-73*	F	Cantspa Uranus	Historic Lady	Mr & Mrs J. Taylor	Owner
1978	Dicarl the Hot News	B	28-5-76	F	Ch. Dicarl the Heavyweight	Dicarl Surprizin Sophie	Miss L. Robson	Mrs D. Johnson
1978	Ulrik of Vackyr	D	4-11-74	Br	Int. Ch. Nord Airways Wrangler of Impton	Vituala of Valkyr	Miss M. Jones & Miss T. Williams	Owners
1978	Sherry Sherain of Salpetra	B	28-7-75	F	Sherain Saul	Gowerfield Garrod	Mrs M. Griffiths	Mr & Mrs Anders
1978	Faircrest Easter Wish	B	30-3-75	F	Zeus of Beechfields	Shandiss Sophie of Faircrest	Mr S. Wareing	Mrs Cox
1979	Jafrak Jungle Stalker of Leebendia	B	30-8-75	F	Ch. Dicarl the Heavyweight	Ch. Dicarl the Lioness of Jafrak	Mr & Mrs Benjamin	Mr & Mrs F. Krall

1979								Owners
1979	Ansets Jubilee Boy	26-11-76	D	F	Ansets Drum Major	Shamgret Zeta of Anset	Mr & Mrs S. Pearce	
1979	The Contender of Dicarl	20-9-78	D	F	Ch. The Weight-lifter of Dicarl	Endroma Lucky Loo	Mrs D. Johnson	Mr & Mrs P. Russell
1979	The Granddaughter of Dicarl	30-8-75	B	F	Ch. Dicarl the Heavyweight	Ch. Dicarl the Lioness of Jafrak	Mrs D. Johnson	Mr & Mrs F. Krall
1979	Dicarl the Dreamseller	6-7-77	B	F	Ch. Dicarl the Heavyweight	Dicarl the Groupier	Mrs W. Doyle	Mrs D. Johnson
1979	Walkmyll Jaeger	5-6-77	D	F	Danelaghs Eurus of Walkmyll	Ch. Dorneywood Dahlia of Walkmyll	Mrs F. Lewis	Owner
1979	Stranahan Shan of Walkmyll	26-11-71	B	F	Danelaghs Eurus of Walkmyll	Ch. Beaudane Golden Dawn of Stranahan	Mrs F. Lewis	Mr & Mrs Reay
1979	Auldmoor Iolanthe	24-12-76	B	Br	Ch. Walkmyll Storm	Auldmoor Artemis	Mrs Harris & Mrs Tilley	Mrs A. Harris
1979	Taranmuir Winstons Belle	7-1-76	B	Br	Ch. Graceloves Tomorrows Hope	Timellie Cinova	Mrs Thorndyke	Owner
1979	Czarina v.t. Buitengebeuren of Impton	30-5-77	B	Bl	Ch. Impton Apache	Impton Oneda	Mrs M. Everton	Mrs L. van der Vijer

Year	Name	Sex	Birth	Colour	Sire	Dam	Owner	Breeder
1980	Samani Desert Chief	D	16–8–79	F/Bl mask	Lincoln Winstead von Raseac	Samani Caprice	Mrs E. M. Bacon	Owner
1980	Dicarl the Hotentot	D	28–5–76	F	Ch. Dicarl the Heavyweight	Dicarl Suprizin' Sophie	B. O. Bream & Mrs H. E. Barker	Mrs D. Johnson
1980	Stranahan Shadrak	D	26–11–77	F	Danelaghs Eurus of Walkmyll	Ch. Beaudane Golden Dawn of Stranahan	Mr and Mrs J. M. Reay	Owners
1980	Talana of Helmlake of Kilcroney	D	28–2–75	F	Ch. Helmlake Chico	Leslies Taura v Glenbrae	D. W. Ranhold & Mrs G Lewestcoyne	Miss Benaim
1980	The Wrestler of Dicarl	D	5–6–77	F	Ch. The Weightlifter of Dicarl	Gaymiles Gorgeous	Mrs D. Johnson	S. Verity
1980	Vernlam Maxie of Delwin	D	15–6–78	F/Bl mask	Lincoln Winstead von Raseac	Sherain Shelagh	Mrs G. A. Godwin	W. Cowlam
1980	Helmlake Catarina	B	31–3–76	F	Ch. Bellote Boffin	Ch. Helmlake Mahe	Mrs K. Le Mare & H. Canham	Mrs K. Le Mare
1980	Millpark Kreme Kracker	B	2–10–77	F	Wharflake Konrad	Millpark Pineapple Poll	Mr & Mrs B. Satterley	Mr & Mrs W. A. Spurrin
1980	Dicarl Fancy That	B	14–10–76	F	Ch. Dicarl the Heavyweight	Dicarl the Fancied	Mrs M. F. Bingham	Mr & Mrs Kirby
1980	Dorneywood Damask	B	23–7–76	F	Ch. Clausentum Gulliver	Ch. Oldmanor Maymirth of Dorneywood	Mr D. R. Bluff	Mr & Mrs D. Parish
1980	Dorneywood Diorissimo of Drumview	B	23–7–76	F	Ch. Clausentum Gulliver	Ch. Oldmanor Maymirth of Dorneywood	Mrs M. Ramsey	Mr & Mrs D. Parish

Year	Name	Sex	Date	Colour	Sire	Dam	Breeder	Owner
1980	Dorneywood Electra	B	23-7-78	F	Danelaghs Eurus of Walkmyll	Ch. Oldmanor Maymirth of Dorneywood	Mr & Mrs D. Parish	Owners
1980	Enydelet the Madame	B	31-1-78	F	Ch. The Weightlifter of Dicarl	Ch. Enydelet Pandora Beauty	Mr & Mrs J. Taylor	Owners
1981	Ashville Harvey	D	23-12-75	H	Ch. Helmlake Chico	Ashville Hannah	Mrs A. P. Gillingham	Owner
1981	Dicarl the Interviewer	D	5-4-77	F	Ch. The Weightlifter of Dicarl	Dicarl The Lady Who	C. Griffiths	Mrs D. Johnson
1981	Helmlake Implicable	D	29-8-78	H	Montego of Helmlake	Ch. Helmlake Fancy Fashion	Mrs K. Le Mare	Owner
1981	Sherain Sheik of Danesworth	D	24-12-77	F/Bl mask	Dorneywood Dandylion	Shoona of Sherain	Mrs Alexander	Mrs Edmonds
1981	Dicarl Tendellie	B	6-7-79	F	Ch. The Contender of Dicarl	Ch. The Granddaughter of Dicarl	Mr S. McAlpine	Mrs D. Johnson
1981	Auldmoor Achaea of Addelos	B	23-10-78	F	Airways Optimist of Impton	Auldmoor Artemis	Mr & Mrs A. D. Howard	Mrs Harris
1981	Leenam I'm Mindy	B	11-7-79	F/Bl mask	Walkmyll Oliver of Russara	Couloir the Baroness	Mr & Mrs D. R. Randall	Mrs J. Al-Kudsi
1981	Salpetra Beaful Girl	B	6-6-79	F/Bl mask	Lincoln Winstead von Raseac	Sherry of Sherain of Salpetra	D. Quinn	Owner
1981	Stranahan Serendipity	B	26-11-77	F	Danelaghs Eurus of Walkmyll	Ch. Beaudane Golden Dawn of Stranahan	Mr & Mrs J. M. Reay	Owners

Year	Name	Sex	Birth	Colour	Sire	Dam	Owner	Breeder
1982	Enydelet Super Cool	D	30–9–78	F	Ch. The Weightlifter of Dicarl	Deansfield Golden Louise	A. Tomlin	Mr & Mrs J. Taylor
1982	Falkenburg Arcas	D	1–9–77	H	Montego of Helmlake	Dicarl Eurika of Falkenburg	Mrs M. E. Penny	Owner
1982	Walkmyll Faithful	D	19–9–78	F	Danelaghs Eurus of Walkmyll	Ch. Halemoss Bettina of Walkmyll	Mr & Mrs M. Brown	Mrs F. C. Lewis
1982	The Advocate of Marladane	D	11–9–79	F/Bl mask	Sherain Sauldanti of Marladane	Marladane Sheba	R. Brunning	K. Perera
1982	Daneagle Alexandra	B	9–2–80	F/Bl mask	Archos Angus	Ch. Dorneywood Damask	Mr & Mrs D. R. Bluff	Owners
1982	Daneton Amilia	B	23–4–80	F	Lincoln Winstead von Raseac	Daneton Princess	Mr & Mrs M. Duckworth	Mr & Mrs Butcher
1982	Drumview Treasure Seeker	B	10–5–79	F/Bl mask	Danelaghs Eurus of Walkmyll	Dorneywood Diorissimo of Drumview	Mrs M. Ramsey	Owner
1982	Jafrak Jinger Cookie	B	5–5–79	F	Ch. The Wrestler of Dicarl	Jafrak Jungle Baby	Mr & Mrs J. Krall	Owners
1982	Dicarl the Alliance with Algwynne	D	26–1–81	F	Ch. The Wrestler of Dicarl	Ch. The Grand-daughter of Dicarl	Mr & Mrs A. F. Herbert	Mrs D. Johnson
1983	Carngray King Soloman of Lismear	D	8–4–80	F	Danelaghs Eurus of Walkmyll	Kohoutek Kalypso	Mrs A. Stephens	Mrs A. Jones

Year	Name	Sex	Date	Colour	Sire	Dam	Breeder	Owners
1983	Yaresville Washington	D	13-10-79	H	Helmlake Gitano	Black Pearl of Giojan	Mr & Mrs C. A. Cropley	Owners
1983	Dorneywood Infanta of Lismear	B	1-8-81	F	Walkmyll Torquil	Ch. Dorneywood Debonair	Mrs A. Stephens	Mr & Mrs D. J. Parish
1983	Helmlake Krazy Fashion	B	17-3-80	H	Ch. Helmlake Implicable	Chy an mor Shining Star of Helmlake	Mrs K. Le Mare	Owner
1983	Hotpoints Fortuna of Walkmyll	B	27-11-80		Gerjos Shilo of Airways	Airways Nebula	Mrs F. C. Lewis	Borghild Sorenson
1983	Impton Motile	B	9-9-80	Blue	Gaylord v.t. Buitengebeuren of Impton	Czarina v.t. Buitengebeuren of Impton	Mrs J. M. D. Rice	Mr & Mrs B. M. Everton
1983	Dicarl Guessing Game	B	2-5-80	F	Ch. The Contender of Dicarl	Iguesso of Dicarl	R. Holder	Mrs D. Johnson
1984	Arianne of Auldmoor	B	3-9-81	F/Bl mask	Ch. Samani Desert Chief	Auldmoor Adella	The Hon. Mrs N. Young	Miss A. M. Hartley & Mrs S. P. Holmes
1984	Devarro Direct Descendant	D	17-1-82	Br	Devarro Director Bains	Dicarl the Autumn of Devarro	Mr & Mrs E. Talbot	Mr & Mrs S. G. Burton
1984	Dicarl the Lady in Waiting at Jalus	B	2-4-80	F	Ch. The Weightlifter of Dicarl	Dicarl The Lady Who	J. Luscott	Mrs D. M. Johnson
1984	Picanbil Pericles	D	3-9-81	Br	Ch. Samani Desert Chief	Auldmoor Adella	Miss A. M. Hartley & Mrs S. P. Holmes	Owners

Year	Name	Sex	Birth	Colour	Sire	Dam	Owner	Breeder
1984	Salpetra Silas	D	24–1–81	F/Bl mask	Lincoln Winstead von Raseac	Ch. Wilgarie Sza Sza of Salpetra	Mr & Mrs P. D. Anders	Owners
1984	Authorpe Hunny Bear	B	31–12–81	F	The Wizard of Dicarl	Hot Cake of Dicarl	Mrs A. E. Goldthorpe	Owner
1984	Cid Campeador de los Madronales of Helmlake Span. Ch.	D	28–2–80	F	Ferro Span, Ch.	Astori de los Madronales Span. Ch.	Mrs K. le Mare	D. Iglesias & D. del Rio
1984	Lismear Accolade	D	17–1–82	F	Tarus El-Hambra	Tresylyan Corin of Lismear	Mrs A. Stephens	Owner
1984	Walkmyll Trestarragon	D	8–9–81	F	Danelaghs Helmund of Walkmyll	Ch. Stranahan Shan of Walkmyll	Mrs F. C. Lewis	Owner
1984	Ansetts The Smoothie	D	12–7–83	F	Ansetts Timekeeper	Waterwoods Ballyhoo of Ansett	Mrs A. E. & Mrs H. D. Pearce	Owners
1985	Batworth Shanghai Lill	B	16–5–82	Br	Macho Man Sunshine Parkers of Helmlake	Taru of Helmlake and Batworth	Messrs Otto and Pakarinen	Owners
1985	Devarro Mister Sullivan	D	11–7–83	Br	Devarro Director Bains	Dicarl The Autumn of Devarro	Mr & Mrs T. Botterill	Mr & Mrs J. G. Burton
1985	Dicarl Crying Time	B	21–9–82	F	The Dicarl Who Watts	I Guess So of Dicarl	M. Simmons	Mrs D. Johnson
1985	She's Sophie of Dicarl	B	2–2–84	F	Unmistakably of Dicarl	Plain Sailing of Dicarl	Mr & Mrs W. W. Hills	Mrs A. Warrick & A. Durrant

1985	Walkmyll Montgomery	D	29-8-80	F	Ch. Walkmyll Jaegar	Ch. Stranahan Shan of Walkmyll	Mrs J. Christie	Mrs F. C. Lewis
1985	Yaresville Westminster	D	31-1-83	H	Ch. Yaresville Washington	Yaresville Black Bubbles	Mr & Mrs A. Cropley	Owners

GLOSSARY

ANUS The back passage through which the contents of the bowels are eliminated.

APPLE HEAD A round, domed head, which is disliked.

BALANCED Every part harmonising; symmetry.

BARREL RIBS Rib-cage excessively rounded so as to prevent the forelegs and elbows being correctly placed.

BITE The front teeth when the jaw is closed.

BLACK A recognised colour of the Great Dane.

BLAZE A white line extending from the skull to the muzzle.

BLOOM Glossiness of coat.

BONE A well-boned dog is one with ample, strong, straight bone, but not inclining in any way to coarseness.

BOSSY A dog which is too heavy in shoulder.

BLUE One of the recognised colours of Great Danes.

BRACE Two dogs of the same breed.

BRINDLE A mixture of light and dark hairs—usually giving a striped appearance, as in a tiger.

BRISKET The chest between the forelegs and beneath the withers.

BUTTERFLY NOSE A black or liver-coloured nose speckled with pink.

CANINE TEETH The long fangs, one each side of the jaw.

CAT FOOT Thick, rounded, tightly closed foot, and thickly padded—resembling that of a cat.

CHALLENGE CERTIFICATE (c.c.) Often commonly referred to as a 'ticket'. An award granted by the Kennel Club for the best exhibit of each sex in a breed at a Championship Show.

CHAMPION A dog which has won three Challenge Certificates, awarded by three different judges, is entitled to the title of 'champion'.

CHAMPIONSHIP SHOW One at which the Kennel Club grant Challenge Certificates for competition.

CHARACTER A dog which combines personality, good temperament, and the traditional traits of the breed.

CHEST The upper part of the body enclosed by the ribs.

CHISELLING The angles dividing the skull and foreface, which should be well defined.

CLOSE-COUPLED Short in the back and loin.

COBBY Thick set.

CONFORMATION The way in which the parts of the body are put together as a balanced whole.

CONGENITAL A feature which is present at birth.

COW-HOCKS Hocks that turn inwards, weak hocks.

CREST The arch of the nape of the neck—much admired.

CROUP The point at which the tail is set on. A steep croup is undesirable.

CRUFT'S The largest dog show in the world, held in London.

CRYPTORCHID A male in which neither of the two testicles is externally visible or functional. Not acceptable for showing under Kennel Club Rules.

DAM The female parent of puppies.

DEW CLAWS Extra 'toes', complete with claws, set well above the feet on the inside of the fore and occasionally on the hind legs. Usually removed a few days after birth.

DISH-FACE A concave muzzle—disliked.

DOWN-FACED The opposite of 'dish-faced'. Also undesirable.

DONKEY STRIPE A dark stripe running down the centre of the back in fawn and brindle puppies a few days old.

DRY Clean skin formation. Sometimes used when defining the neck.

DUDLEY NOSE Light-coloured liver nose. A fault.

ELBOW The joint at the top of the foreleg, next to the body.

EWE NECK A thin, excessively arched, proportionately overlong neck.

EXHIBITOR'S PASS Admission ticket sent by all dog shows to exhibitors.

FANG A large canine tooth.

FAWN One of the recognised colours of Great Danes.

FIDDLE FRONT A crooked front with legs out at elbow and sloping towards each other at the pastern joints, bent forearms, front feet turning outwards. Usually associated with bad rearing.

FLANK The part of the side between the hips and the ribs.

FLECKED Coat lightly ticked as sometimes seen in harlequins. Not desirable.

FLY-EARS Ears that are carried incorrectly instead of lying close to the head.

FLYER An outstanding specimen of the breed.

FOREARM The long bone of the front leg.

FOREFACE The muzzle.

FRONT The chest and forelegs as seen directly from the front of the dog.

GAY TAIL   Tail carried higher over the back than desired, or very curly.

GENES   The units of inheritance.

GOOSE-RUMP   Steep croup, common in the breed, but undesirable.

HACKNEY ACTION   The exaggerated lifting of the legs in the manner of the hackney horse—undesirable.

HARE-FOOT   A long, oval shaped, narrow foot—undesirable.

HARLEQUIN   Black patches on a white ground which predominates. A recognised colour of the Great Dane.

HAW   The third eyelid of the dog. When this is visible, it is unsightly and undesirable.

HEAT   Common term for the season or oestrum of the bitch.

HEIGHT   The height of a dog is measured from a point between the shoulder-blades at the highest point of the slope where the neck joins the back, referred as the withers.

HOCK   The lower joint of the hind leg.

IN-BREEDING   The mating of closely related dogs, i.e. sire and daughter, dam and son, or brother and sister.

KENNEL CLUB   The governing body under whose patronage the world of pedigree dogs operates.

KNUCKLE-OVER   Forelegs which bulge frontwards at the pastern joint are said to 'knuckle over'.

LEGGY   Too high on the leg.

LINE-BREEDING   The mating of dogs of similar families or strains, not too closely related, such as those sharing a common grand-parent, etc.

LIPPY   Lips longer, fuller, or more pendulous than desired.

LOADED   Used in relation to shoulders when they are too heavy. Over-padded with muscle and/or flesh.

LOINS   The part of the body between the hip-bone and the ribs.

LUMBER   Superfluous flesh.

MASK   The dark muzzle of a lighter body colour. Associated with brindles and fawns.

MENDELISM   A theory of breeding.

MERLE   A blue-grey colour, often marbled with black splotches. Not acceptable for showing.

MIS-MARKED   A dog which does not conform to the colour standard.

MOLAR TOOTH   One of the smaller, grinding teeth towards the back of the jaw.

MONORCHID A male animal with only one testicle in the scrotum. Monorchidism is a disqualification under Kennel Club rules and such animals are not eligible for exhibition.

MUZZLE The foreface.

OCCIPUT The peak of the skull between the ears.

OESTRUM The period, or season, during which a bitch may be mated. Usually occurs every six months.

OUT-AT-ELBOW Shoulder-blades loosely attached to the body, jutting out. Usually combined with loose elbows, and often with excessive width between the front legs.

OUT-CROSS The mating of completely unrelated dogs but of the same breed.

OVERSHOT A short lower jaw, or teeth arranged so that the upper set project forward over lower teeth.

PACING Unco-ordinated movement.

PAD The tough sole of a dog's foot.

PADDLING A faulty gait, whereby the front legs are thrown outwards in a loose, unco-ordinated manner.

PART BREEDING TERMS Usually a contract between a breeder and a buyer of a dog or bitch. The terms to be drafted by the interested parties. It is advisable to have agreements such as this put into writing and signed by the parties concerned.

PASTERN The small section of the front leg that joins the foot to the forearm.

PATELLA The knee cap. A small bone situated in front of the stifle.

PAW The foot.

PEDIGREE A register of ancestors; genealogy.

PERIOD OF GESTATION The length of time taken by a bitch after mating to produce a litter—sixty-three days.

PREFIX Consists of words added before the dog's name, in order to identify him with a particular breed or kennel.

PREMOLAR TOOTH The small teeth placed between the large canines and molars or large back teeth. Premolars are sometimes absent, such absence being considered a fault.

PUPPY A dog not exceeding twelve months of age.

QUARANTINE Dogs imported into the British Isles from any country excepting Eire, the Isle of Man or the Channel Islands are required to spend eight months' quarantine at premises approved by the Ministry of Agriculture and Fisheries. Certain other countries have quarantine restrictions and when exporting one should enquire from the Ministry as to the restrictions governing the country concerned.

QUARTERS   Hind legs.

RABBIT FOOT   A flat foot lacking arched toes.

RACY   Light in build and Greyhound in appearance.

RECOGNISED SHOWS   Those held by permission of the Kennel Club and under their rules. Showing at unrecognised shows earns disqualification from any recognised shows.

RIBBED UP   Well 'ribbed up' is a term used for a dog whose ribs are neither too long nor too wide apart, giving it a compact appearance.

RICKETS   A disease of the bones caused by malnutrition, lack of vitamins, dark or damp kennelling, lack of sunlight and fresh air.

RING TAIL   A tail curled over the back, touching the back.

ROACHED BACK   An arched spine.

SCISSOR BITE   Teeth which fit closely, the upper set sliding just in front of the lower set—the correct bite.

SECOND THIGH   The hind leg between the stifle and the hock-joint.

SERVICE   A mating.

SHELLY   Lightly built, lacking bone and substance.

SICKLE HOCKS   Hocks overbent, therefore making the hocks weak.

SLAB SIDES   Very flat sides with insufficient spring of ribs.

SNIPY   Narrow, slight, pointed muzzle. Weak foreface.

SPECIALIST SHOWS   Shows confined to one particular breed.

SPLAY FOOT   A foot with loose, badly fitting toes with space between them.

STIFLE   The joint immediately above the hock corresponding to the knee in man.

STOP   The section between the eyes and dividing forehead and muzzle.

STRAIGHT HOCKS   A lack of angulation, affecting also the stifle, generally causing poor propulsion and choppy movement.

STRAIGHT SHOULDERS   Shoulder-blades too upright, resulting in restricted forward reach of the front legs when moving.

STUD DOG   A male dog for use in breeding.

SWAY BACK   A weak, dipping back.

THROATY   Possessing too much loose skin beneath the chin.

TUCK-UP   A well-drawn-up belly.

UNDERSHOT   The lower teeth, or jaw, projecting beyond the upper teeth or jaw.

UPPER ARM The section between the elbow and the point of the shoulder bone.

WEAVING Plaiting the front legs in action.

WEEDY Lacking bones and substance.

WITHERS The highest point at the neck and shoulder juncture.

BIBLIOGRAPHY

BECKER, FREDERICK. *The Great Dane*, Our Dogs Publishing Co. Ltd. N/D.

BOOKER, BERYL LEE. *Great Danes of Today*, Watmoughs Ltd. N/D.

DENLINGER, MILO. *The Complete Great Dane*, Denlingers, U.S.A. 1950.

EDWARDS, SYDENHAM, *Cynographia Britannica*, 1800.

FIENNES, RICHARD AND ALICE. *The National History of the Dog*, Weidenfeld and Nicolson, 1968.

IDSTONE. *The Dog,* Cassell, Petter, Galpin. N/D.

KECKLER, VIRGINIA. *The Great Dane*, Judy Publishing Co., Chicago, 1953.

LANNING, JEAN. *Great Danes*, W. & G. Foyle Ltd., 1961 (third edition 1968).

LEE, RAWDON. *Modern Dogs (Sporting Division)* (fourth edition), Vol. 1, Horace Cox, 1893.

Leighton's New Book of the Dog. Cassell & Co. Ltd., 1907.

MACKENZIE, DR. MOREL. *Great Danes Past and Present* (third edition), Our Dogs Publishing Co. Ltd. N/D.

SHAW, VERE. *The Encyclopaedia of the Kennel*, Routledge, 1913.

STABLES, GORDON. *Our Friend the Dog*, R. N. Dean & Son. 1884.

STONEHENGE, *The Dog in Health and Disease* (fourth edition), Longmans Green and Co., 1887.

WATSON, JAMES. *The Dog Book*, Heinemann, 1906.

The Great Dane Club Year Books
The Great Dane Breeders Year Books
Deutscher Doggen Club, Vol. 1, 1888–96.
The Great Dane Club of America Diamond Jubilee Year Book, 1889–1964.

INDEX